In honor of my parents,
Gabrielle and Malcolm Cosgrove,
who instilled in me
a love for Israel and the Jewish people,
the ability to think critically,
and the importance of always putting family first

Do not imagine that you, of all Jews, will escape with your life by being in the king's palace. On the contrary, if you keep silent in this moment, relief and deliverance will come to the Jews from another quarter, while you and your father's house will perish. And who knows, perhaps you have attained to royal position for such a time as this.

(Esther 4:13–14)

CONTENTS

INTRODUCTION

The Wake-Up Call

October 7, 2023

"Are you going to get that?"

It was the third time I heard the buzz of Debbie's phone from her side of the bed. As an observant Jewish household, we abstain from using the phone on Shabbat. As a congregational rabbi, I will get the occasional emergency call about pastoral duties that require my attention on the Jewish day of rest. But for my wife, Debbie, to receive a predawn call on Shabbat was unprecedented.

It was her sister Nancy, calling from Israel. There had been an attack—the extent of which was still unknown. The Israeli air-raid sirens had sent everyone into the bomb shelters, and there were scattered reports of an infiltration from the Gaza Strip. Nancy's nineteen-year-old son, Yonatan, was home for the weekend from his military service and had been called back to return immediately to his tank unit. I listened to Debbie's hushed side of the exchange between sisters. "Tell Yonatan we love him," I called out, "and are proud of him."

In the hours, days, and weeks to follow, we would learn not only the extent of the horrors but also their duration. This was not a single or scattered rocket attack to which

Israel and its Iron Dome defense had grown accustomed. This was not the work of an isolated, lone-wolf terrorist, apprehended or "eliminated" by the Israeli Defense Forces (IDF). Beginning at 6:30 a.m., a barrage of over three thousand rockets was fired against Israel, continuing throughout the day. Nearly three thousand Hamas militants infiltrated Israel by land, sea, and air. They breached Israeli security in about sixty locations—a terrorist assault including acts of murder, rape, and hostage taking. It would take hours, amid the chaos and confusion, for Israel to launch a counterattack—hours we now know were filled with horror after horror.

My clergy colleagues and I assembled in synagogue earlier than usual that day. There was both a bar and a bat mitzvah that Shabbat morning, and it was also the penultimate day of the fall Jewish holiday season: a season beginning with Rosh Hashanah, the Jewish New Year, followed by Yom Kippur, the Day of Atonement, followed by the festival of Sukkot (Feast of Tabernacles), and culminating in Sh'mini Atzeret and then Simchat Torah—days given over to appreciating the blessings of life and the renewal of the Torah reading cycle, darkly ironic considering the events unfolding in Israel. There would be special holiday prayers to recite, including a memorial service known as yizkor. How would we negotiate the logistics and emotions of the sacred day with the knowledge that horrific events were developing in real time, happening to our Jewish community halfway around the world? We huddled for a few minutes, then decided that the service must go on, hoping that both our congregants and the Good Lord above would forgive any missteps we made as we muddled through a very fluid situation.

With one exception, the morning passed without incident. Midway through the service, an agitated man whom I did not recognize stepped up to my pulpit. Given the tensions of the day, not to mention recent memories of synagogue attacks in Pittsburgh, Poway, and Colleyville, the exchange was, in retrospect, very scary. Park Avenue Synagogue is a "high-profile community"; a flagship congregation of two thousand member families in Manhattan, with tens of thousands of online participants. Israel was attacked, we could be a target, too—did this individual intend harm to me and my community? Thank goodness, the man was well-intentioned. He too had woken up to the news from Israel. Knowing that not all rabbis would be checking their phones on Shabbat, he had taken it upon himself to visit as many synagogues as he could, to make sure that everyone knew what he knew—that Israel and, by extension, the Jewish people were under assault. The gentleman left as quickly as he arrived—I have never seen him again. After that incident, however, I have made sure that a plainclothes police officer is sitting among my congregation in the pews.

The events of the next few days remain a blur. There were constant calls and text updates from my family and my wife's family who live in Israel. As a clergy team we closed out the Jewish holiday season, celebrating the renewal of the annual Torah reading cycle while keeping tabs on the news from abroad. Twenty-five years into my rabbinate, I have learned to cherish a few days of rest following the holidays. The weeks of anticipation and preparation, and then the officiation of holiday services, are grueling for clergy, and we all look forward to catching our breath at the end of the festival cycle. In the wake of the attacks, there would be no such reprieve. The lives of clergy, mine included, would be turned upside down by the shock of the attacks, Israel's immediate declaration of war, and the first signs of response in America. In the week that followed (and before any Israeli counterattacks), over 150 anti-Israel rallies were held across the United States; incredibly, participants voiced solidarity with Hamas—they viewed the attackers as freedom fighters and their actions as expressions of armed resistance. It felt, and in some ways continues to feel, like we were playing defense and offense at the same time.

I spent hours in dialogue with my colleagues, my synagogue leadership, and representatives of the wider Jewish and civic community to formulate a response and consider possible domestic threats to Jewish interests. Together with other Jewish leaders I stood at the side of a variety of city representatives as they affirmed their support for Israel. Our community rallied to raise funds to help with disaster relief there—breaking an $18 million goal in less than a week. This effort reflected extraordinary community engagement and more phone calls than I can count.

And all this on top of the already frenetic life of a congregational rabbi.

I recall counseling a young engaged couple, planning to wed that week, that despite the news, their wedding must absolutely take place. I shared with them the wise Talmudic counsel that in the event that one must choose between a wedding procession and a funeral procession, the wedding procession takes precedence. Under the cloud of war, as I officiated at their beautiful wedding, I explained to the couple, their guests, and, if I'm honest, to myself that Judaism is a tradition that affirms life. Even, and perhaps especially, in the face of loss, as the biblical book of Deuteronomy states, we are obligated to "choose life."

Having led my congregation through the challenges of the COVID-19 global pandemic, which disrupted our way of communal worship and prayer, October 7th brought with it a feeling of déjà vu: our entire world was turned upside down in an instant. In the wake of the attacks, my congregants, like the rest of the Jewish world, entered an intense period of grieving, with many seeking out me and my colleagues for support and guidance. Yet another layer was added to my normal, overflowing docket of life cycle events—weddings, births, deaths, and hospital visits. One of the challenges of being clergy is the balancing act of supporting a congregation through loss, whether it be the death of a congregant, a global pandemic, or an attack on Israel, while experiencing that loss oneself. Congregants become friends, sometimes best friends, and when they die, a part of me dies. It is not easy to hold another's pain when one is in pain oneself. So too with global events.

For me—and for many Jews outside of Israel—the attacks of October 7th were deeply personal. Was my nephew Yonatan okay? Which of my cousins were being called up to military service? Israel is more than an essential aspect of my identity; it is family—and it was under attack. I had a cousin who was due to give birth, an aunt undergoing chemotherapy. How do these life events happen in times of war? With constant WhatsApp messages from my Israeli family hitting my phone, my mind was understandably elsewhere. And . . . I had a congregation to lead. In the days that followed, I would remind my congregation that "we are traumatized, but we are not paralyzed." I was speaking as much to myself as I was speaking to them.

In hindsight, that predawn wake-up call Debbie received from her sister was a wake-up call for all of diaspora Jewry. We did not understand it at the time, but that morning our eyes opened to a world very different from the one we had gone to sleep in the night before. My life changed that day: my roles as pastor, preacher, and institutional leader took on new urgency and dimension. I became a "wartime rabbi," as my friend Steve (and later, a newspaper headline) would reflect a few weeks into the conflict.

One particular phone call stands out in my mind. Sometime in the weeks following October 7th, my friend Caryn called me and said something to this effect: "Elliot, the whole world was turned upside down on October 7th, and I can only imagine, as rabbi to Park Avenue Synagogue, how your life has changed! The Jewish people are in need of leadership, and you occupy the pulpit of a major synagogue in the heart of the largest diaspora Jewish community. I can't help but think that you didn't choose this moment—it chose you. Who knows, maybe it was for such a time as this that you are in your position." I remember the deep breath I took as the weight of Caryn's words registered.

For such a time as this . . . Whether Caryn knew it or not, she was quoting from the biblical book of Esther. Specifically, the scene in which Queen Esther's foster father, Mordecai, calls upon her to step up and save the Jews of ancient Persia from destruction. Esther does not choose her moment; it chooses her. She is being asked to rise to the occasion. The exchange between Mordecai and Esther is a turning point, not just in the biblical story but in *all* our stories. There is a happenstance nature to our lives—far more is beyond our control than within it. What we can shape, however, is our response to whatever is happening to us. Mordecai's words to Esther (and Caryn's to me) are a reminder of the role of human agency in an out-of-control world often filled with pain. "For such a time as this" is a phrase that has called to many of us, myself included, in the months following October 7th, and the title of this book.

IT WASN'T JUST my world that changed in the months following October 7th—it changed for everyone. The great awakening was not just the trauma of the attack itself, or the war that ensued, or the ongoing plight of the hostages—over 250 initially reported taken captive. That in itself, as the Passover seder song goes, would be "dayenu," "enough." It was more than that—much more.

Jewry worldwide shared a disorienting experience of whiplash—the world was revealed to be less hospitable to us than we had hitherto believed. Our heightened sense of vulnerability spurred a great awakening of individual and collective Jewish identity. In our communities, homes, social media feeds, and hearts, new questions bubbled up to the surface. Was the Israel previously believed to be the powerful, Abraham Accord–signing, tech powerhouse "Start-Up Nation" now exposed as a fragile and, God forbid, fleeting project? From January through October of 2023, mass protests and counterprotests took place across Israel over the government's proposed legislation for judicial reform. About half of the Israeli electorate and much of American Jewry stood at odds with the Israeli government, believing its push for judicial reform was in breach of its founding vision of being both a democratic and Jewish state. Prior to October 7th there existed two radically different visions of the Jewish state, in Israel and the diaspora—Israel's internal rift was thought to be as dangerous as any external threat. Following October 7th, the state and the Jewish community at large came together in unity, however tenuous, to defend Israel against a shared enemy and to face an existential crisis. How do we turn on a dime to defend the wartime decisions of the very government that yesterday was thought to threaten Israel's long-term vitality? And as we watched, the war in Israel set off a flurry of anti-Israel (and often antisemitic) protests in the United States and created a climate of hostility for many Jews across large cities and college campuses nationwide. We also wondered—where did all this antisemitism come from? Was it always there, under the surface, or was a new hatred emerging?

And what did this mean for Jews and our collective iden-

tity? Suddenly, many felt called to be more openly Jewish and proud of their identity, even as they experienced
growing anxiety at the rise of hate around us. Was this the
echo of our parents' and grandparents' experiences as they
escaped from countless pogroms and Holocaust Europe? Is
our identity shaped by the positive "pull" of everything that
brings us together or the negative "push" from others that
sets us apart? Are American Jews members of the privileged establishment or a vulnerable and detested minority?
Where does our Jewish identity end and our attachment
to Israel begin, and what are diaspora Jewry's obligations
to Israel?

In light of the brutality of the October 7th attacks and
the continued plight of the hostages, how is it possible that
a victimized country has come to be portrayed as an aggressor? That even as the fate of the hostages remains uncertain, calls for the destruction of Israel have migrated
from Hamas's founding charter to the chants of university students, side chats, and academic conferences? How
is it possible that an America insistent that Black Lives,
LGBTQ+ Lives, and Asian Lives Matter cannot bring itself to declare that Jewish Lives Matter? How can diaspora
Jewry square the circle of its hope for Palestinian-Israeli
coexistence with the inhuman hatred that Hamas's terrorists inflicted on Israelis on October 7th?

Prior to October 7th, I publicly advocated for a two-state
solution, believing as I still do that everyone—Israelis and
Palestinians—deserves a place to call home. How can we
defend Israel's right to self-defense and self-determination
yet also mourn the loss of every Palestinian displaced, in-

jured, or killed? In a time of war, how do we display empathy for the "other side"? Is it possible to prosecute a war and advocate for peace at one and the same time? In a world divided between "us" and "them," what concerns must I have for the innocent noncombatants among "them," and how do I give those concerns expression?

As many have noted and perhaps as Israel's enemies intended, the October 7th attacks took place almost exactly fifty years after the 1973 Yom Kippur War—a surprise attack by Arab armies that left Israel's fate hanging in the balance. Israel survived that war, but it shattered what Israelis referred to as the *conceptzia,* the hubristic belief that the Arabs could not and would not go to war against Israel. In 1973, diaspora Jewry underwent a transformation, a surge in tribal identity prompted by solidarity with a threatened Israel and a surge in domestic antisemitism. Fifty years later, the Hamas attacks once again shattered Israel's self-perception, sending its political and defense establishment into a painful process of self-examination— how did it fail to protect its citizenry that day?

So too, off the battlefield and across the ocean, diaspora Jewry is asking a host of questions regarding our own condition—questions that extend beyond any single news cycle and run deep into the core of our being. Attendance at worship services and adult education classes, youth group participation, philanthropy, volunteerism—by any metric, there is a surge in Jewish engagement. Jews worldwide are yet again singing the defiant and affirming anthem of our people's solidarity: "Am Yisrael Chai," "The People of Israel Live."

"Amazing / How everything looks / Unchanged, / Even / When nothing / Remains / The same," writes the contemporary Hebrew poet Michael Zats. Here is the paradox of October 7th. At one and the same time, everything and nothing changed: the intractable Palestinian-Israeli conflict and cycle of violence, the blurred line between anti-Zionism and antisemitism, the balancing act by which American Jews bridge all our hyphenated identities— universal-particular, liberal-parochial, religious-secular. These tensions are not new to the Jewish experience.

The pogrom-like nature of the day was intended as and understood to be an attack not just on Israel but on global Jewry. The trauma of the October 7th attacks was not just their brutality but the way they triggered a nerve buried deep in the Jewish psyche, which spurs us to compare a current crisis to past calamities: "The most Jews killed in a single day since the Yom Kippur War . . . since the Kishinev pogroms . . . since the Holocaust." Why did every Israeli or Jewish journalist need to invoke some past Jewish catastrophe as the measuring stick by which to calculate the magnitude of the present one? Whether used intentionally or not, this choice of language is a "code signal," an inner Jewish nod to an idea expressed in this saying attributed to Mark Twain: "While history may not repeat itself, it does rhyme." Or, as the biblical book of Ecclesiastes said so long ago: "There is nothing new under the sun." Indeed, to Jewish senior citizens, especially members of the Holocaust survivor community, October 7th is a trauma beyond words. To have lived this long, to have survived, and . . . it begins again. Israel's back is against the wall, the world's oldest hatred—antisemitism—is still very much alive, and world Jewry feels exposed and isolated once again.

To a younger generation living in the West, who had experienced great freedoms, comfort, and opportunities and were raised to believe in Israel's strength, security, and solidarity, October 7th was a bucket of cold water over the head. We had to suddenly reconsider whatever we may have said to ourselves about Jewish acceptance, about our ability to effortlessly balance the Enlightenment promise of being both a Jew and a secular citizen, and whatever we or the world told us about Jews being members of the "powerful" not the "powerless." Shortly after the attacks, a successful thirty-something-year-old entrepreneur raised on Manhattan's Upper East Side scheduled an appointment with me. He entered my office as if coming to a priest for confession. "Rabbi," he said, "all those stories my parents raised me on—about antisemitism and the importance of Israel—I thought they were delusional. Now I think it was me, not them, who was delusional."

To an older generation with more connective tissue to the Holocaust and the wars of 1967 and 1973, October 7th was a big "I told you so." "In every generation," the text of the Passover seder teaches, "an enemy arises to destroy us." "It was good going while it lasted," they said, in reference to the postwar decades of American-Jewish advancement, assimilation, and acceptance—made all the more so with the pride-inducing backdrop of a sovereign Jewish state. For the older generation, the attacks of October 7th were nothing but a return to the familiar cadences of Jewish history—persecutions, pogroms—a dark cycle going as far back as ancient Egypt and the biblical Pharaoh himself.

So who is right? Is the wake-up call of October 7th the opening of a new chapter in Jewish history, or merely the opening of our eyes to the reality of the world in which we live? At the risk of invoking the cliché about my rabbinic vocation, here's my answer: "both." The questions embedded in the soul of contemporary Jewry long preceded the present crisis. Our attachments to one another, to others, to our Judaism, and to Israel have been negotiated for decades, for centuries, and sometimes for millennia—all the way back to the origins of our sacred texts. Twenty-five years into my rabbinate, I bear daily witness to the generational hopes of the Jewish people, the lived tensions playing out in the lives of contemporary Jewry; as a student of Jewish history, I ask, "How did we get here?" That is the focus of the first part of this book.

Part Two examines the present moment: "Where are we now?" Though prompted by the events of October 7th and their aftermath, I do not focus solely on the day itself; the details, and how to understand them, continue to unfold and are better covered by journalists. Instead, in the pages ahead we'll see that as shocking as October 7th and its reverberations may be, it is best understood as an accelerant or catalyst—not something entirely new. All the fault lines—relations between Israel and diaspora Jewry, antisemitism, the double consciousness of American Jews—have long been with us. October 7th brought them into full relief and gave them new urgency. When seeking to make meaning of catastrophe—Jewish or otherwise—it is wise to be circumspect. There is no silver lining. The sheer brutality of that day, the loss of first Israeli and then Palestinian life caution against any armchair "in crisis there is opportunity" mentality. If anything, in asking "Where are we now?" the second part of this book seeks to place an exclamation point to the first part. We do ourselves no favors by sweeping the challenges facing American and world Jewry under the rug. Part Two seeks to help us navigate the present landscape—honestly, critically, and sometimes painfully.

Ever the preacher, I offer in Part Three prescriptive steps for our journey forward: "Where do we go from here?" Is this a time to circle the wagons or build bridges? Shall we be defined by others' hatred or by the positive pull of living vital Jewish lives? What does the future hold for diaspora Jewry's relationship with Israel? How shall we address the threats from within and beyond the Jewish community, and most important of all, how shall we learn to house the plurality of voices that makes up the symphony of the Jewish people? This story cannot be tied up neatly in a bow. Not so much for any tidy resolutions offered, but in identifying the critical conversations facing American Jewry. It proposes a vocabulary for the work ahead to create a loving, informed, civil, and respectful Jewish communal future.

A note on the subtitle of this book, "On Being Jewish Today": Modest as the global Jewish population may be, there is no presumption that the lived Jewish experience is uniform. "Being Jewish" means different things to different Jews. Not just the variations between religious and nonreligious, Sephardic and Ashkenazi Jews, or, for that matter, political leanings. The lived experience of a Jew (and Zionist) in New York City (where I live) is different from that of a Jew in Savannah or Berkeley. Such an observation holds true even more so in Israel, where Jewish identity does not fall into tidy categories. Israeli Jewry is constituted by a mélange of Ashkenazi, Mizrahi, Egyptian, Yemenite, Russian, and Ethiopian Jewries whose children and grandchildren are marrying each other with increasing frequency, giving rise to new definitions of what it means to be Jewish. "Being Jewish" has never been a monolithic experience in Israel or America—nor is it today. I note from the outset that this book is written from one particular vantage point—my own.

Dealing as this book does with the evolving relationship between diaspora and Israeli Jewry, an additional note on nomenclature—both stylistic and substantive. While American Jewry may be the most numerically significant contemporary diaspora Jewish community, it is but one of many. There are profound differences in what "being Jewish" means in London, Los Angeles, São Paulo, and Sydney. As a first-generation American with family alive and well in Europe, I am well aware that the assumptions, anxieties, and insecurities of American Jews are different from those of our global Jewish counterparts—always, and especially, in fraught times such as ours. Israel's place, functionally, politically, religiously, and otherwise, is decidedly different for American Jews than it is for the rest of diaspora Jewry. My observations on contemporary Jewry, while often applicable beyond American shores, are decidedly American in orientation. Knowing they are not one and the same, I recognize the limitation of alternating between "American Jewry" and "diaspora Jewry." However imperfectly I navigate this difference in the pages ahead, I also hope it alerts readers in diverse locales to a key question on the docket of Jewish peoplehood. Namely, how does my experience of "being Jewish today" intersect with and diverge from that of other members of my global Jewish family?

A final word about timing. I am writing this book as global events actively unfold; therefore its publication will take place in the wake of events that have yet to occur. "I am not," as the biblical Amos preached, "a prophet or the son of a prophet." My primary focus is where we are and how we got here, and not what the unknown future will bring. In providing a vocabulary of understanding and comfort and suggesting some guiding principles, I hope this book will help us navigate any number of possible futures.

We can all feel empowered by Esther's heroism. Her courage lay not merely in the choices she made, but in her decision to be an agent in shaping the future of her people. Her leadership moment, and all "Esther moments" since, can be measured by the degree to which we cease to be bystanders and take action. If this book inspires you, the reader, to step up and play an active role in the unfolding drama of our people in such a time as this, it will have been well worth the effort.

PART ONE

What Was

ONE

LIVING THE HYPHEN

The Heart of Jewish Identity

To live a hyphenated life is not an outcome or destination, it is a perpetual state of being. It means that life is a balancing act between the competing commitments within each of us. We are all composite creations; nobody is any "one" thing. Irish-American, evangelical Christian, Jewish-American—our race, religion, ethnicity, sexuality, nationality, and so many other markers of identity are set in a dialogue, one with the others. Sometimes complementary, oftentimes at odds. A case in point is Queen Esther herself. Woman, Jew, Persian, and queen—her story is a negotiation between her multiple selves.

The challenge and opportunity of American Jewry is situated on the hyphen at the heart of our identity.

Our attachments to one another, to our Judaism, and to Israel require delicate balancing acts, a lifetime of negotiations taking place within our hearts, homes, and global community. The foods we eat, the observances we keep, the people we marry, the loyalties we hold—every decision is shaped by the push and pull originating in this hyphen.

Reflecting back on my earliest Jewish memories, I well understood that authenticity of identity—mine or anyone else's—would be found not so much in loyalty to one side of the hyphen or the other, but in the embrace of each aspect of our identity. It would be in that struggle that a full and fully Jewish life was to be found.

One such example is Shabbat, the Jewish day of rest as prescribed by the Torah and described by Rabbi Abraham Joshua Heschel as a "palace in time." A traditional Jew is called upon to rest on the seventh day, as did God upon the conclusion of the first week of creation.

According to Jewish law, Shabbat begins at sundown—or, as the sages of the Talmud legislated, eighteen minutes before sundown—a built-in buffer to safeguard the sanctity of the seventh day. According to the law of the Cosgrove home in Southern California, in which I grew up, Shabbat began not with sundown, or eighteen minutes earlier, but with the sound of our front door opening and closing, signaling my father's return from work and that the presence of his four sons, with shoes on and collared shirts (as befitted the standards of my English mother), was expected at the dinner table. My mother would kindle the Sabbath lights, my father would bless me and my brothers, and together we would recite the prayers over wine and challah. Dinner conversation ranged from the school week gone by to the latest on the Los Angeles Dodgers and the weekly Torah reading. A hardworking physician, my father had a schedule that was at the mercy of his patients. On any given Saturday morning, he might arrive at synagogue having already done early morning hospital rounds. In the

Cosgrove household, Shabbat functionally ended not with sundown on Saturday, as strict observance would dictate, but when my father got up from lunch to return to the hospital. Holy as the Sabbath was, we children all understood that life was a balancing act.

And the hyphen was lived not just by my father, and it concerned more than medical matters of life and death. As I was growing up, baseball was a religion for me, and though synagogue attendance was mandatory, I often played an early morning game of baseball beforehand. It was understood that the moment the game ended we were expected in synagogue. I have distinct memories of kneeling during the penultimate "aleinu" prayer in synagogue while adjusting my baseball stirrups as they poked out from under my slacks. There were lines of Shabbat not to be crossed, yet others that at times allowed an exception. Certain aspects of Shabbat were sacrosanct, and others were flexible. I recall a dramatic showdown between my older brother and my parents when they forbade him to attend the "final" farewell concert of the rock band The Who because it fell on a Friday night. (Who knew that they would still be playing, decades later!) I remember a different type of example, when my other older brother, the one who excelled at baseball, made the state championships. Not only did my parents give him their blessing to play on Friday night; the whole family was there to cheer him on.

Traditional as our home was, it did not follow the letter of the law. Our Shabbat observance, our dietary observances, the schools and summer camps my brothers and I attended, the girls we dated—pretty much every aspect of life involved a negotiation between our Jewish and secular selves, an expression of our Jewish-American hyphenated identity. Sometimes the balance tipped one way, sometimes the other, and sometimes a third way might emerge that sought to reconcile our Jewish and secular lives. But no matter the outcome, it was understood that every decision would be processed by way of the razor-thin hyphen embedded within each of us.

American Jews are heirs to a twofold spiritual patrimony, American and Jewish. To live a hyphenated life is to engage in a dynamic and sometimes disorienting struggle to integrate these selves. Not just between baseball stardom and synagogue attendance, but all our competing commitments—secular and religious, universal and particular, individualistic and communitarian. Having chosen not to live in insular enclaves, nor, for that matter, to shed the Jewish aspect of our being, life becomes a series of decisions: the communities we join, the schools we attend, the politics we hold, the causes we support, the homes we establish, and much, much more. Choices must be made—we cannot do it all—life is a negotiation.

American Jews, to be sure, are not the first to wrestle with hyphenated identities. Before World War II, the German-Jewish philosopher Franz Rosenzweig spoke of *Zweistromland*, a land of two rivers: "the Jew resides on the banks of two cultures, that of the world and that of Judaism . . . a dual allegiance . . . that preserves the Jew's integrity as both a Jew and a citizen of the world." The sociologist and activist W.E.B. Du Bois, in describing the "two-ness" of the Black community, wrote of "two souls, two thoughts, two un-reconciled strivings; two warring ideals in one dark body." In the Western context, the ideals and the tensions of a hyphenated Jewish identity were probably best expressed by Rabbi Abraham Joshua Heschel, who described American Jews as a people "who live within the language and culture of a twentieth-century nation, are exposed to its challenge, its doubts and its allurements, and at the same time insist upon the preservation of Jewish authenticity."

By a certain telling, this struggle dates back to the first diaspora Jewish community, created when Jacob and his sons leave Canaan for Egypt to eventually be reunited with Joseph at the end of the book of Genesis. While the terms of Joseph's arrival in Egypt are hardly optimal (his brothers sell him into slavery), he goes on to do well for himself. He rises in prominence to become second only to Pharaoh. He dresses, speaks, and walks like an Egyptian, and he raises two Egyptian sons, Ephraim and Manasseh. Reconciled with his family, Joseph cares for them into the twilight years of Jacob's life. On his deathbed, Jacob calls for his grandsons to be brought to him for a final blessing, and they are so assimilated into Egyptian culture, Jacob does not immediately recognize them, asking "*Mi eleh?*" ("Who are they?") The grandsons assure their dying grandfather that despite their appearance, they will remain true to their heritage. To this day, the blessing over the children said by Jewish parents on Sabbath eve recalls this scene. It gives voice to the fundamental hope that our children and grandchildren will be able to "live the hyphen" of being both Jews and participants in secular culture.

To live with a hyphenated identity is a delicate juggling act, a dynamic and sometimes disorienting struggle to integrate our multiple selves. This tension is exemplified by an apocryphal exchange between the US secretary of state Henry Kissinger and the Israeli prime minister Golda Meir. Kissinger informed the prime minister that he was first an American and then a Jew. To which she replied, "That's fine, because in Israel we read from right to left."

The story of American Jewry is largely the tale of the two million Jews who immigrated to America around the turn of the twentieth century in search of a better life for themselves and their descendants. The Jewish story is but one of many tales of hyphenated American populations—about twenty million immigrants arrived on American shores between 1880 and 1920. In the words of a late great historian of American immigration, Oscar Handlin, "Once I thought to write a history of the immigrants in America. Then I discovered that the immigrants *were* American history."

It was in this context that Israel Zangwill (1864–1926) wrote his famous play *The Melting-Pot*. First performed in 1908, it portrays the love story between two young Russian immigrants in America. David is an aspiring Jewish composer, and Vera is Christian—not only that, but also the daughter of the tsarist officer who directed the pogrom that forced David's family to flee Russia. Despite the obstacles that separate them, the New World love shared between David and Vera transcends the hatreds of the Old—it is an inspiring vision of cultural assimilation.

Despite the play's critical acclaim, Zangwill's work was

not warmly received by all. Rabbi Judah Magnes, then the rabbi of Temple Emanu-El on Manhattan's Upper East Side, preached a fiery sermon against Zangwill, arguing that his utopian vision essentially demanded that Jewish-Americans shed their particular identity in the name of brotherhood and progress. Inspired by Magnes, the public intellectual Horace Kallen offered an alternative image—an America that retains *and* celebrates our differences and diversity, an orchestral vision whereby "every type of instrument has its specific timbre and tonality." Kallen never used the word *multiculturalism,* and neither Zangwill nor Kallen were necessarily thinking beyond "white" America, but looking back on twentieth-century social history, clearly it was Kallen (in response to Zangwill) who set the terms of identity politics in this country for decades to come. What was the American dream? Zangwill's vision of acceptance, assimilation, and integration, or Kallen's orchestral vision of Americans, Jewish-Americans included, living out the fullness of their hyphenated identities?

So who won the argument, Zangwill or Kallen? What course of action did American Jews choose? Over the past hundred-plus years, the American Jewish story has been one of integration, assimilation, often upward mobility, and, it seemed, attainment of a long-coveted acceptance. We, our children, and our grandchildren have assumed that no real stigma is associated with being Jewish, that the animus directed at the Jewish people is minimal to nonexistent. Once upon a time, being Jewish was an impediment to social advancement—there were quotas at Ivy League universities, discriminatory hiring practices, and explicit and implicit barriers of access to certain neighbor-hoods and social clubs. Part of the reason, I knew, why my parents came to America was that early in his career, my father was overlooked for a promotion in Scotland on account of his being a Jew. Not the case anymore. Jews have gone from being "the other" to "just another." From the first families of our nation right down to our own—the most interesting thing to say about being a Jew (or marry-ing a Jew) is just how uninteresting it became. Net-net this is a good change, but it comes with consequences.

As the late Eugene Borowitz noted in his book *The Mask Jews Wear*, American Jews had become "Marra-nos in reverse." Marranos were Jews of fourteenth- and fifteenth-century Spain, who under persecution converted to Catholicism but secretly maintained steadfast Jewish practices. The comforts of American Jewry meant we ex-perienced just the opposite: we could publicly affirm our Jewish identities, but we lived at a remove from their well-spring.

This was the "bargain" that American and, largely, much of Western diaspora Jewry have made with modernity. We gained much by entering secular society, but in doing so often shed the distinctive elements of our individual and group identity. In our assimilated comforts, we lost our ability to articulate the hyphen within. In the words of the historian Salo Baron, "What is good for Jews is not neces-sarily good for Judaism." We may know what it means to be an American, we may even know what it means to be a Jew, but we have forgotten that the essence of who we are is not one or the other, but rather the dynamic tension

between the two—the vital and reciprocal exchange between aspects of ourselves that compete and conflict, yet
hold out the possibility of being mutually enriching. This
process can be modeled in our own lives and passed down
from one generation to the next.

The choices my wife and I have made in raising our own
children differ from those my parents made, concerning
the balancing act of dueling identities. I recall the agonizing decision as to whether one of my children would attend secular or Jewish high school and the long, honest
discussions about it—not just between me and my wife,
but with my son, so that he understood the full implications of the choice. Another one of my kids was a very
talented gymnast, so talented that she faced the prospect
of competing on Shabbat. There were lots of tears in our
household—on all sides—as we navigated that decision.
What we eat, what we do, and with whom we do it: our
world does not lack for secular commitments that conflict
with Jewish ones.

Often it is not what we say, but what we ourselves *do,*
that communicates the biggest message. Our children
pick up on our behavior. They see what we snack on, the
amount of time we spend looking at our own phones, and
the manner in which we relate to our spouses and other
adults. They "see" whether we are kind, charitable, patient,
health-conscious, hardworking, community-minded—or
not. They also "see" the Jewish choices we make: whether
we are engaged with the Jewish community, Israel, and
our tradition, whether we aspire to live engaged Jewish
lives. There are no guarantees of success in the transmis-

sion of Jewish identity from one generation to the next, but the role parents play is vital.

I often think of the archetypal "four children" at our Passover seder table, the ceremonial dinner that marks and celebrates our annual festival of freedom: the wise child, the wicked child, the simple child, and the one too young to ask. The most interesting by far is the second child, who asks his parents, "What does this service mean to you?" This child isn't "wicked" as the Passover Haggadah describes him; his question is honest. If we can't provide an answer, by our words and our deeds, as to what being Jewish means to us, then how in the world can children be expected to construct an answer for themselves?

I opened this chapter with my family's peculiar observance of Shabbat when I was a child. I make no claim that the model of my parents, or any set of parents, is perfect. Indeed, one of the great gifts—and burdens—of becoming a parent is recognizing the all-too-human choices of one's own parents and knowing that it is now you making these decisions for your own home. Grateful as I am for the home I grew up in, my imperfect choices are different from those of my parents.

My children have all left the nest now, but throughout their childhood we would conclude every Shabbat at nightfall with the recitation of the havdalah prayer. *Havdalah* means "separation"; it is the blessing that marks the distinction between the Sabbath and the rest of the week, the difference between the sacred and the profane, night and day, the seventh day and the other six, and the Jewish people and the rest of the world. It is a beautiful and beautifully countercultural blessing—a reminder of the balancing act of being Jewish, in how we construct time, community, and other markers of identity. As my wife leads the prayer and we hold hands with our children, singing, we are meant to imagine an ideal, perhaps even utopian vision of the world as it could be. The language of havdalah is decidedly not some sort of John Lennon–esque imagined vision in which the world will "live as one," as all our differences blend into one great melting pot. It is, rather, a vision whereby the Jewish people, and all people, can live peaceably together, amid their differences. A vision of tribalism without triumphalism, affiliation without parochialism, peoplehood without ethnocentrism. A language and lifestyle of havdalah, of Jewish difference and distinction appropriate for our age.

It is not easy. In fact, it is a very narrow path to walk. But it is upon that narrow hyphen of our identities that we will find our way toward actualizing the potentialities of our contemporary Jewish lives.

TWO

THE INVISIBLE THREAD

Jewish Faith and Our Ancestral Homeland

"Here lies the righteous champion of Torah, our rabbi and teacher Yekutiel Aaron, son of Rabbi Moshe Kozlovsky of blessed memory who served in the sanctified vocation of shochet [ritual slaughterer] in London for decades under the authority of the Rabbinical Court. Cherished for his faith and pure fear of God."

O f all the commitments embedded within the Jewish soul, perhaps the most enduring concerns the land of Israel. An invisible string connects it to our hearts. The story of my great-grandfather, Yekutiel Aaron Kozlovsky, offers one modest example of the Jewish people's intergenerational attachment to our ancestral land.

The earliest physical artifact of my family history is his headstone in the cemetery on the Mount of Olives in Jerusalem; its inscription opens this chapter. Born in Vilna, Lithuania, in 1860, Yekutiel Aaron (known as Aaron) married my great-grandmother Sarah and together with their three daughters immigrated to the United Kingdom, participants in the great westward migration of Eastern European Jewry in the last quarter of the nineteenth century (Aaron's older brother Zev had already arrived in Brooklyn, New York). For reasons unknown, Sarah and Aaron settled in Pennycraig, Wales, a small mining town where my grandfather Kenneth was born. According to family lore, Sarah, "Momma Kozlovsky," insisted that the family leave South Wales in order to raise the family in London, where Aaron would spend his career serving the Jewish community as a shochet (ritual slaughterer) and mohel (one who performs ritual circumcisions).

Having successfully raised their children, in the last decade of their lives Aaron and Sarah fulfilled their life-long dream of immigrating to their ancestral homeland. Deeply religious, my great-grandparents longed to live, die, and be buried in the land of their forefathers. Shortly after my grandparents were married, in 1932, Aaron and Sarah made aliyah (meaning they immigrated, or literally "ascended") to what was then Mandatory Palestine under British rule. Considering the hardships and costs associated with travel, Aaron and Sarah's journey to Palestine was understood to be a one-way ticket. Today, as a parent, and hopefully future grandparent, who feels the deep attachment between generations, I am struck that the gravitational pull my great-grandparents must have felt toward Palestine was strong enough to make them bid farewell to their family, knowing they would likely never go back to London. Indeed, Aaron and Sarah would never meet their grandchildren—my father and his brother. The onset of

World War II made travel between the UK and Palestine all but impossible. Aaron and Sarah lived the remainder of their lives in Tel Aviv and died in 1940 and 1943, respectively. They were buried in Jerusalem's Mount of Olives cemetery, where, according to Jewish belief, the resurrection of the dead will begin when the Messiah arrives.

When Israel was established in 1948, Jerusalem was divided in two, and the Mount of Olives fell under Jordanian control. With the reunification of Jerusalem following the 1967 Six-Day War, my grandfather, who had changed his surname from Kozlovsky to Cosgrove and spent his entire career as a congregational rabbi in Glasgow, Scotland, was finally able to visit the now badly damaged graves of his parents.

I never knew my grandfather; my arrival to and his departure from this world took place at around the same time. I can only imagine what it must have felt like for him to pay his respects at the final resting place of his parents, to whom he had bid farewell nearly forty years earlier. To see where his parents were buried, on the holy ground of the Mount of Olives, in a Jerusalem that was now the capital of the sovereign State of Israel—it was not the arrival of the Messiah, but as I imagine it for my grandfather, it must have been a profoundly redemptive moment.

As long as Jews have been Jews, we have been connected to the land of Israel. God's initial promise to the biblical patriarch Abraham is threefold—descendants ("like the stars in the sky and sand of the earth"), blessing ("and you shall be a blessing"), and land ("the place that I will show you"). A connection to the land is woven into the fabric of our faith. The narratives of the biblical patriarchs and matriarchs are motivated by their anxieties about leaving the land and their desire to return to it. My great-grandparents' end-of-life aspiration to be buried in Israel finds precedent in the book of Genesis itself. Upon hearing the news that his beloved son Joseph is alive and well outside the land, Jacob descends to Egypt to be reunited with his son and lives out the rest of his days there. Years later, on his deathbed, having blessed his family, Jacob adjures his children to see that he is buried in the land of Canaan, a commandment that they fulfill. Joseph similarly requests that his remains be brought to the Promised Land, a request that Moses' successor, Joshua, will fulfill, after the hundreds of years that the Israelites live enslaved in Egypt, then wander in the wilderness.

FOR THE TWO thousand years of exile following the destruction of the Second Temple in Jerusalem in 70 CE, the thoughts, prayers, and rituals of the Jewish people have been directed toward Israel. Our psalms of joy and lamentation ("If I forget thee, O Jerusalem"), the ministries of our great prophets (Isaiah, Jeremiah, Ezekiel) can all be read as an extended meditation on the Jewish connection to the land. The prayers we pray, the direction in which we pray, the breaking of a glass at Jewish weddings (to commemorate the destruction of the Temple), the pledge of "Next year in Jerusalem" that ends the Passover seder—all are rituals that tie us to the land. No matter where we live, the gaze of our eyes and the devotion of hearts are directed toward Zion—the biblical designation for Jerusalem and God's holy and eternal dwelling place. Judaism is a faith, a peoplehood, and a ritual practice, but it is also a connection to a place—the land of Israel.

The paradox, of course, is that for much of Jewish history (since the fall of Jerusalem to the Romans in 70 CE), the vast majority of the Jewish people has been exiled from the land. Yet in good times and bad, be it in Babylonia, Lithuania, North Africa, or New York, our spiritual posture has always been directed toward Jerusalem. "My heart is in the east, and I am at the ends of the west," wrote the twelfth-century poet Judah Halevi from Spain. We lived wherever we lived, but implicit in being a Jew was a self-understanding that our spiritual self would find its greatest fulfillment in Israel. Whether we are Jewish-Spanish, Jewish-British, or Jewish-American, our connection to and hoped-for return to Zion is the most persistently shared aspect of our multi-millennial journey. And while some Jews have always lived in Palestine—and others, like my great-grandparents, chose to die and be buried there after residing elsewhere—all Jews hold Zion in their hearts. Jewish identity has always been measured by way of geographical and theological proximity to the land, the irony being that a faith so anchored to the land was, historically speaking, developed outside the land—we were a landless people with a land-centered faith until 1948.

When Israel's first prime minister, David Ben-Gurion, established the State of Israel on May 14, 1948, it was both a culmination of and a break with thousands of years of Jewish history. This moment did not come by way of prayers and miracles, but by the blood, sweat, and tears of generations of Jews who, beginning in the 1880s, worked toward making the multi-millennial dream of Jewish sovereignty a reality: "To be a free people in our land," as Israel's national anthem, "Hatikvah," declares. No longer second-class or persecuted residents of host countries, Jews found, in the State of Israel, the opportunity to be the subject of their own sentence rather than the object of someone else's. What does a state look like if its military, health care system, and sanitation department are informed by Jewish values? How would Israel reconcile its commitments to being both the Jewish state and a liberal democracy? How would the Jewish experience of having lived as a minority in the countries of the diaspora inform Israel's treatment of the Arab minority in its midst? How would Israel address the fact that its own claim to the land stands in conflict with another people's claim to it—the "hidden question" asked by Zionist thinkers like Yitzhak Epstein as early as 1907? It had been two thousand years since Jews had a country of their own—a very long time since they'd had to ask these questions, and asking them continues to shape what Israel is and will be. The adage "One campaigns in poetry and governs in prose" has held true in the realization of the Zionist dream. On May 14, 1948, the challenging work of state building began among a people no longer in exile.

Transformative as 1948 was for the Jews who lived in Israel, the establishment of the new state raised a host of new questions for those who did not. Whatever hopes the ideologues and founders may have harbored about the voluntary ingathering of the Jewish people, that vision did not materialize. While the arrival of thousands of Holocaust refugees from displaced persons camps and the involuntary immigration of hundreds of thousands of Jews expelled from Arab lands (Egypt, Iraq, Yemen, Libya, and elsewhere) boosted Israel's population in its early years, by contrast the vast majority of American Jewry stayed put.

Nevertheless, for them, the founding of the sovereign Jewish state changed their status. Why? Because as of May 14, 1948, the Jew in New York, Los Angeles, or Miami was no longer "in exile," but in the diaspora.

Israel was no longer a theological abstraction. How would diaspora Jews orient themselves to the living, breathing Jewish state when they opted not to live there? Prior to May 14, 1948, the term "Israel" referred to the entire people of Israel, wherever they might dwell. Following May 14, 1948, as Ben-Gurion would make clear, Israel became a specific geographic and political designation.

The uncharted relationship between diaspora Jewry and Israel has raised all sorts of questions concerning nomenclature, theology, and realpolitik. Is diaspora Jewry now excluded from the name and destiny of "Israel"? Do those of us with no intention of uprooting ourselves to live in the Holy Land still pray for the "ingathering of exiles"? How does a Jew living in Moscow, Milan, or Milwaukee support the Jewish state while remaining a proud citizen of their own country of residence and citizenship? Up until 1948, Zionism, loosely defined, stood for supporting efforts to establish the Jewish state in the land of Israel. What is the

new definition of Zionism for the person who has chosen
to opt out of settling in the land? To what degree may,
or must, a diaspora Jew engage with, support, defend, or
critique the actions of the Jewish state—one that, no different from any other, makes both good and bad choices?
Is Israel the Jewish state, or the state of the Jews—all
Jews—wherever they may be? If the latter, what does that
concept mean in practice?

Israel's founding had profound implications for the self-
perception of diaspora Jews. Established soon after the
horrors of World War II, Israel, at its most basic level, provides refuge for world Jewry, should they need it. Never
again would Jews, as was the case in the Holocaust, be denied safe harbor from their oppressors. But Israel was more
than that. In diaspora hearts and minds, it was a source of
pride: a new and more assertive identity that served as a
counterpoint to the vulnerability of the Holocaust and the
thousands of years of pogrom-filled exile that preceded it.
While opting out of living in Israel, diaspora Jews derived
vicarious confidence as the first stages of Israel's existence
unfolded. Whether we were safer because Israel existed or
not was beside the point—we felt safer because we lived in
a time of a Jewish state.

An uncharted relationship between diaspora Jewry and
Israel was filled with all sorts of new questions; I take comfort in the thought that ours is not the first generation to ask
them. Toward the end of forty years of wandering in the
Sinai, the children of Israel prepare to enter the Promised
Land. The tribes of Reuben and Gad approach Moses and
the chieftains of Israel to ask if they can be excused from

continuing on. As cattle holders, they prefer to settle in the grazing land east of the Jordan River. Whatever the merits of their request, Moses, understandably, goes dark: "Are your brothers to go to war while you stay here? Why will you turn the minds of the Israelites from crossing into the land that the Lord had given them?" (Numbers 32:6–7).

Moses is outraged that these tribes are sidestepping the call, dating back to Abraham, to enter the land, *and* also prioritizing a comfortable existence for themselves while their brethren fight. Moses further understands that the choices of these two tribes could affect the temperament of the rest of the people: "Why should we put our lives at risk while our brothers live in ease outside the land?"

Eventually, a settlement is brokered. The request of the tribes is granted, contingent on their agreement to be *halutzim* (shock troops), fighting at the vanguard of Israel's forces. When, and only when, Israel has successfully settled in the land will they be able to return to their livestock, wives, children, in the land east of the Jordan.

THIS EXCHANGE IN the book of Numbers is the first, but not the final, memorandum of understanding negotiated between Jews in the diaspora and Jews in the land of Israel. Though we live in times vastly different than those of the Bible, the terms of that first settlement continue to be negotiated. In Israel's brief history, the relationship between diaspora and Israeli Jewry has been much debated, and continues to be. In 1950, Ben-Gurion and David Blaustein, the president of the American Jewish Committee, agreed that Ben-Gurion would both tone down his calls for diaspora emigration and refrain from intervening in American Jewish life. In exchange, Blaustein (speaking on behalf of American Jewry) stated that while American Jewry could offer advice, cooperation, and help, it would not attempt to speak in the name of other Jewish communities—Israel included.

The importance of the Ben-Gurion–Blaustein agreement is not so much its durability, but rather that it is a benchmark more honored in the breach than in its observance. Ben-Gurion never really stopped telling American Jews not to forget where they belong: in Israel. In March 1960, Moshe Dayan announced that the Israeli government represents not just the people of Israel but the interests of all Jews. That same year, Foreign Minister Golda Meir similarly announced that "Israel will continue to speak for Jewry." The infractions went both ways. In 1992, American Jewish lobbyists infuriated the government of Prime Minister Yitzhak Rabin for having "pushed too hard on the loan guarantees and against arms sales to Arab countries, poisoning the waters between the US administration and Israel." Depending on the issue of the moment, be it the US sale of AWACS (airborne warning and control system) planes to Saudi Arabia, loan guarantees, the preliminary agreements between Israelis and Palestinians known as the Oslo Accords, or, more recently, judicial reform in Israel, Israelis have variously resented and encouraged the activism of American Jewry on their behalf. Time and again, American Jewry has been forced to contend with tensions that the Ben-Gurion–Blaustein agreement—and before that, the agreement between Moses and the breakaway tribes—was, at least in theory, supposed to mitigate.

WHATEVER TENSIONS EXISTED and continued to be negotiated following 1948, American Jewry's engagement with Israel became a constituent building block of American Jewish identity. In the wake of Israel's establishment and the horrors of the Holocaust, non-Zionist expressions of Jewish life (as found in classical Reform Judaism and ultra-Orthodox Jewish sects) were understandably marginalized. Supporting Israel became part of Jewish identity among American and other Western Jews. The pulpit of my synagogue, for example, like so many others, is adorned with an Israeli flag, and the prayer for the State of Israel is central to our liturgy. Curriculum regarding the history of Zionism and modern Israel is integrated into congregational schools, Jewish day schools, and Jewish camping establishments. In times of both comfort and crisis we raised vast sums of money for the nascent state and helped other Jewish communities (in Ethiopia, Russia, Syria, for example) find refuge in the land. Summers in Israel, gap semesters, and gap years became a normative expression of Jewish life. Politically, American Jews were expected to support elected representatives who prioritized the defense of Israel—important in itself but also a rallying cry to unify American Jewry in all its political and religious diversity. As the slogan goes, "Wherever we stand, we stand with Israel." Two of the most impactful achievements of American Jewry over the past half-century are AIPAC, the American Israel Public Affairs Committee, a lobbying group that supports Israel, and Birthright Israel, an organization offering a free ten-day trip to Israel to all Jewish young adults, ages eighteen through twenty-six. Birthright Israel was established in 1999 by philanthropists led by Charles Bronfman and Michael Steinhardt. Both efforts are centered on Israel engagement. Israel has served as the bonding agent keeping American Jewry together.

As I reflect back on my own coming of age as an American Jew, I can see that Israel played a foundational role in shaping my Jewish identity. My first international trip, at the age of eight, to Israel with my father was significant because of the destination and the treasured time for father-son bonding. I have such vivid memories of visiting Jerusalem, Masada, and the Dead Sea. I recall walking through the streets of Tel Aviv, amazed at the spoken Hebrew, the Jewish soldiers, and the possibility of having a kosher hamburger ("McDavid's"). I remember meeting members of my extended family and my father's friends, taken by the thought that I was connected to these people. I remember the night my father dropped me off to stay with my uncle in Tel Aviv; when I woke up in his apartment, his stunning, Hebrew-speaking girlfriend poured me a bowl of cereal. Jewish life in Los Angeles was pretty good, but, in my impressionable mind, Israel represented an alternate universe of bold Jewish empowerment.

That feeling only grew stronger in high school and college, as I participated in summer teen travel programs in

Israel. Navigating around the country with my broken Hebrew, meeting up with family and friends—but more important, feeling that I was part of an extended family—this was thrilling, as was connecting with my Israeli aunts, uncles, cousins, and family friends.

If I had to distill the cumulative effect of all these experiences into a single sentence, it would be the pithy observation I would hear years later from the Israeli prime minister Yair Lapid: "I could be you and you could be me." In meeting my actual Israeli family, together with my extended family in Israel, the secret ingredient of Jewish peoplehood came alive in my heart.

"I COULD BE you and you could be me." Had the one-year visit my British parents made to America over fifty years ago lasted only that one year, I would never have been born in the United States. Had my father taken a faculty position in Israel, I would have grown up in the Mediterranean climate of Israel, not Southern California. And before that, had my great-grandfather in Vilna not decided to flee the tsar's army by going to Wales, of all places, then the Lithuanian Kozlovskys would never have become the Scottish Cosgroves, who would never have become . . . you get the idea. But for the vagaries of history, we could all be in someone else's shoes. This is the foundation of feelings of kinship and, in the case of the Jewish people, the essence of our peoplehood—and for me, my connection to the people and State of Israel.

Indeed, once in college, I engaged in my Judaism not by means of the "religious" dimension of my identity, but rather through my activism on behalf of Israel. I led a campus mission to Washington, DC, for an AIPAC conference, worked as a summer research intern in the AIPAC office in DC, and, following graduation, very nearly took a job working at AIPAC. My decision not to do this, but rather to live in Israel, turned out to be the most important decision of my life. Not just for the love of Israel that year instilled in me, but also for finding the love of my life—my then girlfriend and now wife and mother to my four children. She too was taking a postcollege gap year. Part of the intensity of our courtship was our mutual identification with the land and our shared journey as we both wrestled with the question of immigrating to Israel. That conversation, which started when we were both so young, continues over twenty-five years later, implicitly and explicitly, to this day.

Growing up in our household, our children endured repeated reminders that their parents' love story is anchored in Israel. One day, they too might meet their beloved there. With cousins in Israel and as children of a congregational rabbi, they have been to Israel more times than they can count, forming memories, connections, and friendships of their own. Most of all, our children know that their parents have wrestled with, and *still* wrestle with, the question of whether to live in Israel. On multiple occasions, our family has openly asked whether we should move there—based on principle, profession, or some combination of the two. Our children know that should they decide to move to Israel, they'll have their parents' full support.

∽

ISRAEL IS NOW in the fourth quarter of its first century, and American Jews continue to wrestle with the idea of a Jewish state that is an *extension of,* but not *interchangeable with,* their Jewish identity. American Jewry can rightfully marvel at and support modern Israel, despite the fact that we have opted out of the opportunity to live there.

As for me, no different than my great-grandparents in a bygone era, I maintain every reason to believe that whatever the future holds for me and my wife, our story will ultimately bring us to Israel. I console myself with the thought that my present contributions to American Jewry mitigate my ongoing and unfulfilled aspiration to live in Israel. Like the Israelite tribes who chose not to settle in the land, my identity is nonetheless tied to the well-being of those who have done so. Whatever our personal choices may be, the "tug" toward the land endures. From generation to generation, and all the more so in our own, the pull toward the land of Israel informs the hearts of the Jewish people.

THREE

THE TWO WORLDS
OF JUDAISM

Israel, the Diaspora,
and the Divisions Within

Catastrophic as the attacks of October 7th were (and continue to be) for their immediate victims and the collective psyche of Israel, they also sent shockwaves through the global Jewish soul.

Diaspora Jews whose identities were aligned closely with Israel rallied behind their Hebrew-speaking family who were under attack. They mourned for their Israeli brothers and sisters, recognizing an attack on Jews in Israel as an attack on Jews everywhere. For others, however, whose connection with Israel was more tenuous, the response varied. Many American Jews, though bound to Israel by religious history and a sense of kinship that is perhaps undefined, have a fraught relationship with the Jewish state. This may be because of the policies of the Israeli government, Israel's Chief Rabbinate, and in some cases, even the idea of Jewish sovereignty; for them, Israel has ceased to represent the values of American Jewry—an estrangement that goes both ways.

Long before October 7th, sociologists of world Jewry tracked the widening distance between diaspora and Israeli Jews. While every person of conscience was horrified by the attacks, for diaspora Jews living in a world of Judaism different from that of their Israeli cousins, watching a war unfold halfway around the world raised complex questions about how to contend with day-to-day news out of Israel. How did two such different Jewish communities emerge, and what claims do our very different worlds have upon each other? These are questions at the fulcrum of my life as a rabbi and a Jew, and they are central to many American Jews after October 7th and Israel's response to the massacre.

In considering these questions, I often return to an exchange, or more precisely, a non-exchange that occurred a few years ago. I was standing in line with my daughter at the salad bar of an all-inclusive holiday resort when a man in a bathing suit in front of me bellowed at his son, "Yuval, atah honek et ha-tor!" ("Yuval, you're choking up the line!")

Most diaspora Jews have been in this situation: we overhear a bit of spoken Hebrew in an unexpected place, signaling that an Israeli is in our midst. The diaspora Jew's sense of kinship is triggered. My daughter looked up at me, smiling. She knew that we knew what neither the Israeli man (nor his son) knew—that we all belong to the same people. I am a people person, and he seemed friendly enough; our kids were about the same age, and neither of us had anywhere to go other than our beach chairs. Why not strike up a conversation with my Israeli kinsman? Despite the situation's incredibly low barrier of entry to a social exchange, the truth is, I did and said absolutely nothing, and the moment passed. He never knew what I knew. As for me, I have thought often about the conversation that never occurred.

Do American Jews and Israeli Jews have anything to talk about? We share a history, a faith, and a connection to Israel——Israelis as citizens there, American Jews from afar. The vast majority of world Jewry live in either Israel or the United States; depending on how one counts it, there are seven to eight million Jews in each. I can speak a fumbling Hebrew, I have visited Israel more times than I can count, and I even lived there for extended periods. I advocate on Israel's behalf and, by dint of my day job, I am in contact with a number of elected representatives of the Jewish state. But put me in a bathing suit and stand me next to a secular Israeli around my age and, aside from our receding hairlines and rising cholesterol levels, what connection do we share?

Since its founding, Israel has undergone multiple dramatic transformations——demographic, economic, geopolitical, and otherwise. It has absorbed millions of immigrants from the Arab world, the former Soviet Union, Ethiopia, and elsewhere. Surrounded by hostile neighbors, it has fought multiple wars, emerged onto the world stage as the "Start-Up Nation," and recently has engaged in historic bridge-building diplomacy with the Gulf States. So too, its struggle to come to terms with the Palestinian population within and beyond its borders——in all its political, security, and moral ramifications—continues to be a defining part of what Israel has been, what it is, and what it will become.

As for the Judaism of the Jews of Israel, the realization of a multi-millennial dream of a sovereign Jewish state has included its share of challenges and opportunities. On the one hand, the whole point of Israel was to be a Jewish state. On the other hand, it has sought to enter the community of nations as a liberal democracy. The tension between the two commitments is palpable in Israel's Declaration of Independence, which is both an extended meditation on the Jewish claim to the land as a place for the ingathering of Jewish exiles and an affirmation of Israel's aspiration to be a country ensuring "complete equality of social and political rights to all its inhabitants irrespective of religion, race, or sex . . ."

From Israel's founding documents to the 2023 mass protests over the Netanyahu government's push for judicial reform, there has been a push and a pull in Israel between its two founding impulses. This is complicated by the fact that Israel lacks any equivalent to the American doctrine of separation of church and state. Shortly prior to Israel's founding, for reasons more pragmatic than ideological, Israel's first prime minister, David Ben-Gurion, a secular Jew, extended to the then numerically small ultra-Orthodox Jewish community, by way of the office of the Chief Rabbinate, control over matters related to religious life, such as public transportation on the Sabbath, food supervision, and marriage and divorce. This decision is referred to as the status quo agreement. As the numerical and political strength of Israel's ultra-Orthodox community increased over the decades, so did the scope of its influence. No longer circumscribed to matters of ritual life, the Chief Rabbinate now has sway over matters of school funding, authority over who determines "who is a Jew," control of Jewish holy sites, military exemptions for yeshiva students, and much, much more.

Over many years, for the typical secular Israeli Jew (like my Hebrew-speaking would-be friend at the salad bar), relinquishing control over the Jewish content of the Jewish state was a matter of little consequence. They thought of the Chief Rabbinate and its functionaries merely as a nuisance; in the words of Israeli author Einat Wilf, they were akin to public utilities—present to officiate at weddings and funerals, for example. Though secular Jews viewed the system created by these religious authorities as imperfect and antiquated, they "lived with" or "worked around" it. A fragile détente emerged between Israel's religious and secular communities, the former granting the latter control over matters of governance, the latter ceding control of religious matters to the ultra-Orthodox.

When exactly that balancing act fell apart is a matter of some debate. Some see it as the rise of religious-nationalist ideologies following the 1967 Six-Day War. Others point to the 1977 election of Likud's Menachem Begin and the shifts in power and demographics from Israel's founders to a new generation of leaders. The more assertive religious presence, combined with the minoritarian system of Israel's parliament (the Knesset), whereby smaller coalition partners hold outsized power, brought religious parties to more prominence in Israeli policy and governance. The fault lines in Israeli society—be it the more religious character of the state, the government policies regarding settlements in the West Bank, or the question of control over holy sites, such as the Western Wall—became impossible to ignore. On one side stood a politically and religiously right-leaning "Jerusalem" electorate; on the other, a more westernized secular Hebrew-speaking "Tel Aviv" electorate, which supported liberal democracy.

For me personally, the cracks in the competing visions of Israel's future broke open when I was living in Israel in 1995—the year Prime Minister Yitzhak Rabin was assassinated. For a young rabbinical student, it was an optimistic time. In addition to enjoying my studies in Jerusalem, I could feel a hopeful mood in Israel—peace rallies and back-channel negotiations between sworn enemies suggested that a new political reality was emerging. A legendary military leader and chief of staff of Israel's Defense Forces during the Six-Day War (1967), Rabin had pivoted in his later years, by way of the Oslo Accords, to establish a framework for resolving the Israeli-Palestinian conflict—the "land for peace" agreement. Rabin's assassin was a religious extremist. He justified his deranged actions by asserting his belief that he was saving Jewish lives endangered by Rabin's peacemaking efforts.

I will forever remember where I was when I heard the news of Rabin's murder, and the feeling of shock caused by the fact that it was a Jew who took the prime minister's life. In retrospect, I can see that Rabin's death was not the only one that occurred that day. The vision of Israel that he represented also died. In the decades that followed, Israeli politics took a decidedly rightward turn—the growth of Israel's ultra-Orthodox community, the expansion of the settlements in the West Bank, and the rise of religious extremism all reflect a hardening of Israel's body politic. In the face of two intifadas, bus bombings, rocket attacks, and the rise in Palestinian extremism, Israel's peace camp has more or less crumbled. The physical security wall erected alongside the border dividing Israel from the territories is understood by most Israelis as necessary for Israel's continued security.

EVEN PRIOR TO October 7th, the year 2023 was a defining one for Israel's body politic. On November 1, 2022, Israelis had gone to the voting booth. Although the popular vote was evenly divided, the nature of Israel's parliamentary system of coalition politics brought about a seismic shift. The most right-wing government in Israel's brief history came to power. The governing coalition took a rightward turn on a series of social issues, including, but not limited to, women's and LGBTQ+ rights, religious pluralism, blanket exemptions from military service for the ultra-Orthodox, and settlement construction in the West Bank.

Jarring as this was, it took more than that to bring Israelis out to the streets in protest. This did happen when the new government proposed legislation for judicial reform. Those Knesset members who favored it believed the legislation signaled a long overdue correction to the flaws and imbalances of Israel's judicial system; and, as the democratically elected representatives of the Israeli people, they were well within their right to pass it. Those protesting the proposed changes believed them to be a fundamental threat to Israel's democratic character. Indeed, while the 2023 protests were ostensibly about particular issues such as the selection of judges and judicial override, most everyone agrees that the true underlying issue was far more profound: namely, who will control the present and future governance of the Jewish state and what kind of vision will guide it.

From January through October 2023, mass protests took place across Israel. The millions protesting and counterprotesting on the streets every Saturday night, the military reservists refusing to serve in the IDF, and the unprecedented calls from within Israel for diaspora Jewry to exert pressure—all these things together made one thing clear. A frightening, and frighteningly divided, Israel was emerging.

DRAMATIC AS THE tale of Israeli Jewry has been since its founding, the evolution of American Jewry during these same decades has been no less transformative. Long established in the United States and also transformed by the millions of Eastern Europe immigrants arriving in 1880–1920, American Jewry was further and forever changed by the GI Bill, which after World War II granted veterans access to many levels of university and professional education. Jews had once been excluded from these opportunities, but this was the case no longer, profoundly affecting the young veterans' hopes for the future. American Jews began to leave behind their old neighborhoods, their Old World accents and traditions. Many sought to assimilate, embracing a secular and pluralistic vision of America.

This was "the bargain of the emancipation." Namely, in return for becoming fully integrated citizens, Jews were expected (or expected themselves) to shed their distinctive religious and cultural markers and adopt secular lifestyles. A decline in Jewish religious observance and affiliation was followed by a precipitous rise in intermarriage. Parochial Jewish concerns were replaced by more universal and progressive ones, as exemplified by the ubiquitous phrase "tikkun olam" ("mending the world").

By a certain telling, the distinction between the American "brand" of Judaism and the Israeli one has everything to do with context. Israel's stated goal is to be a Jewish state. But in America, Jewish religious expression is different. Although religious values may, or even ought to, inform the public square, no particular religion can have the upper hand. The separation of church and state ensures that every faith, majority or minority, may practice its faith in any way its followers choose, for those who choose a faith at all.

From this soil grew the many types of American Judaism practiced today: American Orthodox, Conservative, Reform, Reconstructionist, Renewal, Jubus, and more. The promise of America is the promise that you can practice your Judaism as you see fit. In fact, as Americans, we will fight tooth and nail to protect that right. Self-evident as this concept may be to an American Jew, it is altogether foreign to today's religious establishment in Israel, which is controlled by the state-sanctioned, ultra-Orthodox, and increasingly powerful Chief Rabbinate.

As the "Judaism" of American Jewry grew less pronounced, the civic religion of American Jewry grew to take its place. It came to be expressed in the many organizations that serve as the institutional foundation for American Jewish life. They include Jewish Community Centers (JCCs), Jewish social service organizations such as United Jewish Appeal (UJA), and Jewish advocacy groups such as the Anti-Defamation League (ADL) and the American Jewish Committee (AJC). As the incomprehensible horror of six million dead Jews settled in, Holocaust memory and caring for the survivors and their descendants became, appropriately, a communal priority; "Never Again" became a rallying cry against antisemitism and many different abuses of human rights; rituals of remembrance were formalized. The rhythms of the American Jew may not be religious ones, but they reflect a secular religion adapted to American shores.

But more than social service agencies or Holocaust memory, it was engagement with Israel that became the "religion" of American Jews. The culmination of thousands of years of Jewish striving, the establishment of Israel became a badge of honor for American Jews. The horrors of the Holocaust, not to mention the tragic pogroms that populated Jewish history, more than sufficed to prove the need for a sovereign Jewish state and refuge. Whether the presence of Israel made the Jew in New York, Detroit, or San Francisco any safer from the threat of antisemitism was beside the point. By virtue of Israel's existence, American Jews walked taller and believed themselves to be safer. Israel was a pulsating vision of Jewish strength and self-determination.

Israel focused the energies of American Jewry. We were proud of our Israeli cousins and wanted to help them, and the fact that we could provide Israel with philanthropic and political support served their needs and ours. Israel missions, Israel education, Israel advocacy—in good times and bad—became a kind of secular religion for American Jews, sometimes supplanting Judaism itself. It is easier, after all, to write a check than it is to keep our children home on Friday night to light Shabbat candles. Uninspired by the prayerbook, unfamiliar with the Talmud, American Jews became adept at new Jewish topics of conversations—how our elected leaders vote on legislation regarding Israel's security or the terms by which the United States should or shouldn't enter into a deal with Iran. The dividing lines between us no longer fell along the various levels at which we observed the Sabbath or dietary laws, or our beliefs as to whether the Torah is of divine origin. Our views on Israel took the place of these. A new Israel-based religion emerged.

And in some cases, engagement with Israel became more than a religion—it became an orthodoxy. It makes perfect sense that the imperfect policies of Israel (or any state) might be worthy of objection—by Israelis, Israel's Jewish supporters, or anyone—and sensibility has very little to do with it. For an American Jew to suggest that this or that policy of the Israeli government was not in the long-term best interest of Israel came to be understood, in certain circles of the American Jewish establishment, as a form of betrayal. As the late Rabbi Arthur Hertzberg once observed, "The lack of support for Israel [is] the only offense for which Jews can be 'excommunicated.'" Israel, the thinking goes, does not lack for external enemies. Because they have opted out of the opportunity to live in Israel, American Jews must forgo their right to critique Israel because any such criticism will become fodder for Israel's real enemies.

To make matters even more complicated for American Jews, while our Jewish identity obligates us to engage with Israel, it is a religious identity that is not recognized by Israel. American Jewry is undergoing a process of redefinition in which the lines between Jew and non-Jew are becoming increasingly blurred. With over 70 percent of non-Orthodox American Jews marrying someone born of another faith, the future of the American rabbinate (and American Judaism writ large) will be situated on our ability to balance our fealty to Jewish law and lived lives of the Jew-ish families we serve. Some of my Reform colleagues, for instance, readily officiate at interfaith weddings—an opportune touchpoint for a rabbi seeking to shape the faith of that new household. Others, myself included, seek to embrace the would-be marriage partner of a Jew with an approach to conversion as inclusive as possible within the bounds of Jewish law. We may differ in particulars, but the conditions to which we are responding are the same. Namely, how shall the American rabbinate best strengthen the increasingly heterogeneous Jewish community that we have been tasked to serve? And because America, unlike Israel, eschews any notion of a centralized rabbinate, the diversity of responses will undoubtedly increase in the years ahead.

Not so in Israel. There, all matters of personal status (birth, marriage, conversion, burial) fall under the authority of the Chief Rabbinate. So, for instance, when two Jews from the diaspora register to get married in Israel, the Israeli rabbinate requires some sort of letter vouching for the Jewishness of the individuals in question—letters which many American rabbis, Orthodox ones included, are not authorized by Israel to provide. In the eyes of the State of Israel, American Jews are no longer empowered to say "who is a Jew." In other words, our religious identity is not recognized by Israel.

Here lies an irony. Much of my energy is devoted to supporting the Jewish state—which does not recognize the Judaism I teach and preach as Judaism at all. This state of affairs can make American Jews feel that the Israel they love does not love them back, or even care that we exist. I recall the shock and dismay my daughter Maddie shared upon returning from her Israel gap year, discovering that her Israeli peers, in whose condition so much of her Jewish education had been directed, cared little, if at all, for her well-being and that of diaspora Jewry. While I myself may be constitutionally incapable of walking away from Israel, others will continue to do so. There is a limit to the self-flagellating exercise of supporting a state that neither recognizes you nor represents your values. For the coming generation of American Jewry, the loyalties of yesteryear no longer suffice.

And of all the points of difference between the "religion" of American Jewry and the reality of Israel, none loom as large as the Palestinian-Israeli conflict. For the post-Shoah generation of American Jewish leadership, Israel's claim to the land and need for a sovereign state were obvious, a simple matter of survival. In the first decades of Israel's existence, persistent Arab hostilities sidelined any concerns American Jewry might have harbored about the democratic rights of the indigenous Palestinian population. History didn't help—Arabs had long rejected the Jews, and mainstream American Jewry paid little attention to Palestinian aspirations to nationhood, focusing instead on the pressing needs of the Jewish people. Expressions of concern for the Palestinians and the conditions they lived in were beyond the bounds of Jewish communal discussion.

But the past fifty-plus years of Israeli settlement expansion have radically changed the facts on the ground and American Jewry's perception of Israel as a Jewish and a democratic nation. Whether American Jews know about, or care to understand, the events leading up to the Six-Day War, through which Israel gained control of the territories known as the West Bank, here's what matters to them: Israel continues to occupy those territories. Whatever justifications (theological, security-related, or otherwise) have been and continue to be marshaled in support of Israel's ongoing presence there, in the eyes of a liberal-leaning American Jewry, the West Bank settlements and the illiberal policies they represent pose a threat to Israel's founding promise—its commitment to democracy. For American Jewry, it cuts close to the bone to see its most prized liberal value in peril. As the thinking of progressive American Jewry goes, if the project of Israel is to provide a homeland and security to a historically vulnerable Jewish minority, then how can the state not respond to the needs of the vulnerable minority in its midst? Leaving aside the role of historical revisionism and progressive identity politics, the unresolved status of the Palestinians—lacking as they are in freedom of movement and access, self-determination, and other accoutrements of sovereignty—forms a wedge issue between an increasingly liberal-leaning American Jewry and an increasingly right-leaning Israeli Jewry. The mainstreaming of Jewish fundamentalism in Israeli society and government further compounds the problem. The fact that the same government fails to recognize American Jewry and also fails to recognize the Palestinian right to self-determination increases American Jews' sense of estrangement.

For American Jews, to live in the presence of the State of Israel but not actually in Israel reminds us of the choice we have made about where we live and how we define our Jewish lives. When we talk about Israel, we are talking about a Jewish community that defines its existence in a manner fundamentally different from how we define ours. Israeli Jewry is defined by physical borders and national identity. American Jewry is defined by religious borders: the communities we join, the practices we observe, and whom we marry. Israel's border incursions come from Lebanon and Gaza, ours from intermarriage. At age eighteen, many of our children go off to campuses and become educated in the liberal arts and universal values. At eighteen, their children go off to serve in the army and defend a nation. American Jewish identity is a matter of choice and volition; Israeli identity is a matter of necessity and self-preservation. We are animated by different concerns, contexts, and missions.

In other words, a perfect storm has emerged between the two centers of the Jewish world, America and Israel. A loosening definition of Jewish identity in America and a tightening in Israel have come to pass. One Jewry is assimilating rapidly, and the other is becoming parochialized beyond recognition. Each is unsure how invested it really is in the other's well-being.

Oftentimes, when secular Israelis leave Israel to live abroad, they don't attempt to understand or associate with diaspora Jewish life and remain disconnected from American Judaism. Notwithstanding personal and professional relationships, and the personal Jewish practices they may observe (Passover seder, Hanukkah candles, and so on), the institutional life of American Jewry is, more often than not, a foreign concept to the typical expat Israeli. Sometimes they walk into my office when they fall in love with a non-Jew, but for the most part, aside from bumping into them at a local Israeli concert or holiday resort salad bar, odds are that secular Israelis in the diaspora and American Jews are totally disconnected in terms of how we understand and practice our Judaism. My Jewish concerns are not theirs, nor are theirs mine.

What does a liberal American Jew have to say to a secular or ultra-Orthodox Israeli? As it turns out, not much. And when we do speak, more often than not, the two communities speak "at" rather than "to" each other. Israeli Jews view Americans Jews who voice protest against Israeli government policies, be it matters of religious pluralism or settlement expansion, with curiosity and resentment. "You don't live here, pay taxes here, or serve in our military. Why should we care what a diaspora Jew like you thinks?" The resentment runs the other way as well. Be it the latest statement from Israel's minister of interior on who is or isn't a Jew, or the latest decision precluding the possibility of a future Palestinian state—the decisions made by the Jewish state necessarily have an impact on the condition and perception of world Jewry. After October 7th, the news out of Israel has had a profound impact on all of diaspora Jewry. Each movement impacts the other, but like clumsy dance partners, we seem to keep stepping on each other's toes.

STRENGTHENING THE BONDS between the worlds of American and Israeli Jewry is one of the paramount issues facing Judaism today. Efforts must be made in the diaspora and in Israel to find common ground and points of dialogue. We must recognize that while our culture and concerns are far from one and the same, our destinies are tied together. We share a family of origin yet walk this world at a distance. Israel and diaspora Jewry must be vigilant to care for and protect each other, to correct each other when one or the other steps out of line, and to do so in a way that respects our mutual and enduring loyalty.

Though it comes from a very different context, Rainer Maria Rilke's poem "Love Song" captures my own aspirations for the future relationship between Israeli and American Jewry. Rilke depicts the affections of two lovers, separate yet fused together at the soul: "everything that touches us, me and you, touches us together like a violin's bow, which draws one voice out of two separate strings." In good times and in crises, this is the great task of diaspora and Israeli Jewry. Like two distinct strings on a violin, we must find a language that permits us to remain distinct yet produce a unified sound. We remember we are *am ehad*, one people, in dialogue and partnership, equal and passionate stakeholders in a shared destiny.

FOUR

EMPATHY AND VIGILANCE

The Two Responses to Jewish Trauma

I t is a truism of life that suffering is part and parcel to being human. I know this intimately as a pastor to my flock and a student of the human condition. Nobody makes it through this world without experiencing hurt, setback, pain, or hardship. Given this universal and unavoidable feature of our humanity, the only variables are when our suffering will occur and, when it does, how we will respond.

Some respond to victimhood with stoic resilience and perseverance, perhaps a hopeful belief that tomorrow can be better than today. A person has learned the hard way how precarious life is—and therefore treats it as a precious treasure. Nobody should experience hurt as we did—so we respond with acts of kindness and empathy. I recall one late congregant, Rachel, a Holocaust survivor devoted to my adult education classes. She had somehow survived the concentration camps where most of her family had been murdered. Rachel had a love of life and zest for learning—

she met every idea and every person with genuine curiosity and love. "I try to greet every day and every person with kindness," she once told me.

I asked her the obvious question. Given her experiences, given her loss—how did she keep her cheerful demeanor? The focus of her Holocaust memories, she explained, was on the small acts of kindness by which she was able to survive. The non-Jew who hid her at great risk to himself, the shared food ration that kept her from starving, the support that she and her fellow inmates extended one to the other. The kindness of others, not the hatred of her oppressors, influenced her most, sustaining her then and into the years to come. Rachel's life was a modest one; there are no monuments, plaques, or foundations in her name. Yet her decision to live an empathy-filled life was nothing short of heroic.

But empathy and kindness are not the only human responses to suffering. Fear, anger, hatred, and hypervigilance are perhaps more frequently the tools of the victimized. "I have been hurt," says such a person, "and I will never allow myself to be wounded again. My present anger and my hypervigilance against potential future hurt are my response to my fears of victimhood." Again, as a pastor, I see this reaction all the time. Congregants often come to my office with complaints—about me, other congregants, the imperfections in synagogue life (there are many!). As our time together winds down and they reach for the doorknob of my office to exit, often they share an as-yet-unspoken hurt they are carrying—perhaps a financial setback, the grind of caring for an aging parent, the frustrations of an unhappy marriage. Psychological bruises, no different than physical bruises, are tender to the touch, and as humans, we have a system of spoken and unspoken defenses to protect ourselves from further harm. Anger and hatred are the flip side of suffering and victimhood—natural responses to actual or perceived hurt.

Neither response, empathy or anger, is in and of itself right or wrong. Why one response and not the other? It is not for anyone but a particular person—or people—to know, but it makes all the difference in the world.

The Jewish people have experienced more than our fair share of trauma, and this question sits perennially on the Jewish docket: how shall we respond to our individual or collective trauma—past and present? Since the atrocities of October 7, 2023, we wrestle with that question with increased intensity. A terrible hurt has been inflicted on our people—how shall we respond? Ours is not the first Jewish generation to ask the question.

One need look no further than perhaps the most familiar of all Jewish rituals—the Passover seder. Over 70 percent of American Jews take part in this annual meal. *Seder*, which is the Hebrew word for "order," includes the ritualized telling of the ancient Israelite journey from Egyptian bondage under Pharaoh to freedom. Whether religious or secular, an all-night affair or a tale to be quickly dispatched in under thirty minutes, this celebration involves traditional foods and songs and a symposium of questions and answers as Jews come together to tell the biblical story of our liberation from Egypt. The presence of loved ones, the tastes and smells of the holiday meal—the seder is a night to look forward to and a night to remember. Seders can be repositories of nostalgia, a time for family-specific traditions, recipes, and ritual objects passed down from one generation to another. The ancient story of Passover continues to shape Jewish identity. No mere recitation of bygone events, it is a project of meaning-making and identity formation.

At its core, the Passover Haggadah, a liturgical telling of the Exodus story, relays a national saga of trauma. It evokes two different responses—empathy and compassion on the one hand, vigilance and self-defense on the other. The empathy instinct is the better known of our responses to our Exodus from Egypt. We *were* slaves, but now we are free people—instilling in us an attitude of gratitude that must inform our every action. We are overflowing, literally, with thankfulness, singing songs and psalms of praise and thanks. "Dayenu," the most famous of the seder songs, has this refrain: "It would have been enough." We praise God for "over the top" kindness. "Had God only brought us through the sea, fed us with manna, or given us the Torah—dayenu—it would have been enough."

This kind of gratitude leads to empathy for those less fortunate, for those who have not yet experienced liberation. The biblical commandment to be empathetic is stated in the book of Exodus: ". . . thou shalt know the heart of the stranger, for you were once a stranger in a strange land." Passover's remembrance of historical oppression is the driving force behind Jewish empathy to the condition of "the other"—an "Exodus mentality" by which historic Jewish suffering is transformed into compassion. We recognize that while we "are free," others wait for liberation. At our family seders, I recall conversations, readings, and rituals about the plight of Soviet Jewry, Syrian Jewry, or Ethiopian Jews who were still striving for freedom (we also attended marches on their behalf).

Passover's cry for freedom does not end with the parochial boundaries of the Jewish people, however. Our compassion extends beyond the Jewish community: "Let all who are hungry, come and eat," we announce as we sit down to begin the seder. "Let all who are in need, come and share in the Passover meal." The holiday gathering is imbued with an inclusive and universal message that calls on us to set a place—literally and figuratively—for anyone in need. Embedded within the Passover story is a message oriented toward all of humankind. Immigrants on the southern border, refugees around the world, reproductive rights, the LGBTQ+ community—any group of people on the periphery is welcomed into the fold.

One year, I recall, an orange appeared on our Seder table. Why? As goes the urban myth, the great contemporary scholar of Jewish studies Dr. Susannah Heschel was once confronted by a curmudgeonly man who insisted that a woman belongs on a synagogue pulpit as much as an orange belongs on a seder plate—meaning not at all. And thus the feminist tradition and new Jewish ritual of putting an orange on the seder plate began at her seder and then at many others—ours included. We well understood that the historical alienation and oppression of our own people was intended to be leveraged toward concern for all marginalized populations.

Not just Jews, and not just non-Jews, but even our enemies themselves are, according to the seder, the object of our concern. Growing up, I was always deeply impressed at the point when, just before we recited each of the ten plagues, we dipped our finger into our cup and "removed" drops of wine—one for each plague. The reason, I was told, is that even though the Egyptians enslaved us and even though the plagues were necessary for our liberation, we are still saddened at the fact of Egypt's suffering. In our home, we read a Talmudic passage describing the Egyptians' pursuit of the fleeing Israelites and how the Egyptians drowned in the sea. When the heavenly angels broke out in song at the downfall of the Israelites' oppressors, God reprimanded them: "My handiwork [the Egyptians] are drowning in the sea, and you want to sing a song of praise?" So great is the empathy of Passover that we do not rejoice at the fall of our enemy.

Yet the message of Passover also includes words about vigilance and self-defense. In my childhood home, the high point of our seder came not with the searching for the afikoman (the hidden broken matzah, without which the meal cannot conclude), a particular food, the recitation of the four questions, or even—in a household of four boys—the jockeying over who would read which passage regarding the four children. The high point was when our mother sang the Hebrew song from her English childhood known as "V'hi She'amdah." We came to know its loose English translation by heart, by way of my mother's annual recitation of it which she had learned from her mother, my granny. Born in Manchester, England, my mother is a lady in every sense, her British accent as strong today as it was when she arrived in the States decades ago. As warm a person as she is, because of her English reserve she rarely sings in public. So when she did so at our crowded Passover seder table, the room grew quiet with deferential respect. As we arrived at the particular page of the Haggadah, all eyes would turn to her, and these were the words she would sing, an adapted translation of "V'hi She'amdah":

This wonderful old promise, how constant is its power!
It sweetens all our sorrow and brightens each dark hour.
God kept it through the ages, He keeps it firm today.
Though many men are striving to sweep our folk away.
Fierce foes have fought against us in every age and land.
But the Holy One of Israel has saved us from their hand.

Year after year, we children sat in rapt attention during my mother's solo performance, and the power of the moment left a profound impression on me. In recent years, this moment has taken on additional significance as the granddaughters (there are many) now sing backup to their grandmother's lead.

Following the arc of the Jewish historical experience, the couplets track God's abiding promise and presence. Comforting as the words (and melody) may be, the tale they tell is not a pleasant one. Not just God's promise but also the perennial threat of Israel's "fierce foes" (as my mother reached to sing a high D) are invoked. Ancient Egypt's Pharaoh was the first, but by no means the last, in a long line of oppressors who sought to "sweep our folk away." In every "age and land" a new Pharaoh has arisen, and oppression of the Jews has followed. In such a telling, Passover becomes less a story about liberation and more a warning to be vigilant because persecution has pursued the Jewish people since time immemorial. Be it the Egyptians, Babylonians, Greeks, Romans, or Byzantines—the pattern extended into the Middle Ages and the modern period too, from pogrom to pogrom. We Jews must be ever on guard; another Pharaoh is always right around the corner.

Along with the need for vigilance, the seder experience references the desire for vengeance. Toward the end of the seder, at the redemptive moment when we stand up, open the door, and welcome in the peripatetic mystical prophet Elijah, we do so not with words of blessing but with a spite-filled mélange of biblical verses called "Sh'foch Hamat'kha." The passage calls on God "to pour out your divine wrath upon the nations . . . pursue them with anger and destroy them from under the heavens of the Lord." Nobody is quite sure precisely when this tradition actually began. It expresses a desire for divine retribution upon those who cause great suffering. It speaks to the spiteful aspect of the Jewish response to vulnerability. I can only imagine all the dark chapters of Jewish history when Jews sat huddled in their homes, fearful of the world they lived in. The Passover story cut a bit too close to the bone; so for a fleeting second, they opened their doors, thumbed their noses by way of biblical verses at the inhospitable world, and then shut the door quickly, fearful for their lives and the next blood libel or pogrom. We hear their voices for a moment, and remember them.

EMPATHY AND VIGILANCE. Two responses to suffering. The threads woven into our founding fabric that explain both our origins and our present day. Not just in the story of Passover, but in many other stories of our people, we find choices being made between one response or the other. Is the springtime Jewish holiday of Purim (that comes about a month before Passover) meant to be a frivolity-filled festival of light, joy, and gladness? It is celebrated with costume parades, the exchange of gifts, and donations to the needy. But the final chapters of the story of Esther (as we will explore in chapter 10) are not about joy, but vengeance. Having been saved from destruction, the Jews of Shushan take revenge upon their would-be destroyers: "Thus the Jews smote all their enemies with the stroke of the sword, and slaughter and destruction, and did what they would unto those that hated them" (Esther 9:5). By such a telling, the message of Esther becomes a cathartic story of psychological release, produced by a disempowered author imagining what to do to the oppressor if only they had enough power. The remembrance of our victimhood and our resultant hypervigilance is codified into the yearly calendar and the soul of the Jewish people—a subject we will return to soon enough.

Empathy or vigilance? For thousands of years, the question was theoretical. Jews living in exile, fearing their next persecution, were neither positioned to "know the heart of the stranger" nor to defend themselves against the threats they faced. Their concern was appropriately and solely directed toward self-preservation. What heroes did we have to look back on? Stories of brave biblical judges like Deborah and Gideon, or post-biblical Judah Maccabee and his band of Greek-fighting brothers, were far removed from the realities of a disempowered, exiled people.

When we arrived in America, Jews operationalized empathy by establishing social service and self-help agencies aimed at supporting at-risk Jewish populations or advocating for Jewish interests. The founding of the Hebrew Immigrant Aid Society (HIAS, 1881), the American Jewish Committee (1906), the Joint Distribution Committee (1914), and many others reflected the first organizational steps toward an impressive scaffolding of support by which American Jewry could lend aid to Jewish interests worldwide.

As the Jewish community assimilated into its American setting and as Jewish social service agencies found common cause and collaboration with a wider network of secular social service agencies, the emphasis on helping those in need within the Jewish fold expanded to include a much broader humanity. For the first time in a long time, Jews were positioned to put their words into action by way of tikkun olam, "mending the world." Examples of tikkun olam abound: The Philadelphia Hebrew Benevolent Society, founded in 1854, would be renamed the Jewish Family Service, expanding to include the wider community. The ADL, initially founded to combat antisemitism and discrimination against Jews, evolved to combat bigotry of all kinds. HIAS makes the shift explicit in its promotional literature: "We used to take refugees because they were

Jewish. Now we take them because we're Jewish." Organizationally, American Jewry pivoted from particularism to universalism. Over time American Jews became some of the most effective advocates for progressive causes. From feminism to fighting poverty, from the seder to civil rights, from Emma Lazarus to Ruth Bader Ginsburg—three thousand years of Jewish empathy had a platform for expression on American soil.

To be sure, not all American Jews are card-carrying supporters of progressive causes. Not all are liberal in their leanings. For many in the American Jewish establishment, questions of Jewish self-defense remain at the forefront of the agenda. Our fears of antisemitism are based on the real, not the imagined. Look no further than much of the world's reaction to the attacks of October 7th as proof positive of a widespread inhospitable stance toward Jews. Violence against Jews and Jewish institutions, verbal harassment and intimidation have been rising on campus and online. "Fierce foes have fought against us in every age and land": the Passover words as sung by my mother—gentle yet urgent—still relevant.

AS AMERICAN JEWRY'S immigrant story and the contours of its founding ethic took shape, a very different narrative was concurrently developing in late nineteenth-century Palestine. The Jewish people's claim to the land began with God's promise to Abraham in Genesis, chapter 12, but in the late nineteenth century, a painful and

fresh realization of the world's (often deadly) inhospital-
ity to Jews, together with the rise of nationalism, revi-
talized the old millennial dream. Years before Theodor
Herzl wrote his pamphlet "The Jewish State" (1896) in
response to the European antisemitism he witnessed in
his day, the Russian-Polish activist Leon Pinsker penned
"Auto-Emancipation" (1882) in response to the massive
anti-Jewish riots in tsarist Russia in 1881. Not by assimilating into and contributing to their host societies would
Jews realize the promise of emancipation, Pinsker argued;
they needed to assert control of their own destiny by way
of national self-determination. In these same years the first
wave of immigration, or aliyah, arrived in Palestine, which
was then under Ottoman rule. This was the first nascent
effort to establish a Jewish homeland. The immigrants gave
themselves the name BILU, an acronym for Beit Ya'akov
L'khu V'nelkha, "House of Jacob, let us go." Not through
the kindness of strangers, but by doing it for themselves,
would Jews stand tall among the nations.

In no small measure, the evolution of early Zionism
took shape in response to the sufferings of Jews in the
diaspora. Following the 1903 Kishinev pogroms in what
was then Russia, anti-Jewish riots that included looting,
arson, rape, and the murder of some forty-nine Jews,
Chaim Nahman Bialik (1873–1934) was sent by the Jewish
Historical Commission in Odessa to interview survivors.
Bialik, who would later become the preeminent poet of
Modern Hebrew, was asked to prepare a report on the
atrocities. In addition to his report, Bialik wrote an epic
poem called *Ba-ir Ha-ḥariga* (*In the City of Slaughter*). Unlike

his contemporaries, such as Tolstoy and Gorky, who wrote condemnations blaming the Russians or the government, Bialik turned his wrath on a most unlikely group: the Jews themselves. For Bialik and his readers, Kishinev was a symbol of Jewish helplessness: Jews hiding in hovels and holes, praying that they would escape evil as their mothers, wives, and daughters were raped before their very eyes.

Drawing on the history of the Maccabees, the iconic second-century BCE paragons of Jewish bravery who fought their oppressors and established the Hasmonean dynasty, Bialik gave voice to his feelings of shame—his own compatriots did not fight back:

> . . . *the heirs*
> *Of Hasmoneans lay, with trembling knees,*
> *Concealed and cowering—the sons of the Maccabees!*
> *The seed of saints, the scions of the lions!*
> *Who, crammed by scores in all the sanctuaries of their shame,*
> *So sanctified My name!*
> *It was the flight of mice they fled,*
> *The scurrying of roaches was their flight;*
> *They died like dogs, and they were dead!*

Bialik's poem was a watershed literary event for Jews as they considered their relationship to self-defense and power—*In the City of Slaughter* became compulsory reading for the Labor Zionist youth movement. No longer would Jews cower in fear. They must once again become the Maccabees, the few who stood up to the many and overcame them, doing right for the wronged. Never again would Jews be without power, never again would the "New Israeli" submit, as did old Judaism, to exile and powerlessness.

And so it was and so it became. Like any ideology, Zionism comes in a variety of expressions—political, religious, cultural, and beyond. Vladimir Jabotinsky, already shaped by the trauma of the Kishinev pogrom, would, in response to the Tel Hai massacre of 1920, break from the more moderate mainstream Zionist party of Chaim Weizmann to form Betar—an assertive Zionism of self-defense. Tel Hai was a small Jewish settlement in northern Palestine that came under attack by Arab forces and was eventually overrun—one of its defenders, Joseph Trumpeldor, became famous for his last (and perhaps apocryphal) words: "It is good to die for our country." The massacre reinforced Jabotinsky's belief in Jewish self-defense: Betar aimed at educating youth in a militant national spirit. Jabotinsky mobilized Jewish forces of self-defense; his iconic essay, "Iron Wall," urged an uncompromising militancy in the face of Arab opposition to the nascent Jewish state.

And while the establishment of Israel in 1948 put an end to millennia of exiled victimhood, the remembrance of that trauma and vulnerability persists. In Israel's relatively brief history, it has experienced more than its fair share of battles, and the tensions in its national psyche reflect competing responses to the trauma of war. A case in point is the trauma born of Israel's 1973 Yom Kippur War, during which 2,656 soldiers were killed in action, over 12,000 wounded, and hundreds captured, many of them subjected to torture by the enemy. Israel would never be the same:

the shockwaves of the war reverberated through the country into the years to come.

The trauma of the 1973 war gave rise to at least two major movements. Though the ultra-nationalist Orthodox right-wing settler movement, Gush Emunim, technically began in the aftermath of the Six-Day War in 1967, the Yom Kippur War functioned as its major call to action, pressing the issue of Israel's security and territorial integrity. This movement aimed to expand the settlements, a religious and ideological mission informed by a belief, born of trauma, that the territories were vital to Israel's security. On the other side of the ledger, Israel's Peace Now movement also began after the war in 1973. In this case, trauma led many Israelis to reevaluate the costs and consequences of a prolonged conflict; both secular and religious Israelis began advocating for a negotiated settlement based on the principle of "land for peace." (Without this, the statesmanship of Kissinger, Begin, and Sadat might have come to naught.) Thus we have two movements born of a single trauma, representing two diametrically opposed visions of Israel's future—a division that continues to play out to this very day.

As is the case with diaspora Jewry, the tensions within Israel are also situated on questions of the response to trauma. Many (but not all) of Israel's most fractious debates are less about the ostensible issue (settlements, judicial reform) than about deeper questions in Israel's substratum of how Israelis respond to the pain of the wars it has fought, and continues to fight. Shall the hand it reaches out be open and extended or closed into a fist? Shall American Jews define themselves with an inclusive and universal empathy or guard against another spasm of antisemitic hatred dating back to Pharaoh?

Complicating matters, of course, is the debate over categorization: Are Jews privileged or persecuted? Powerful or powerless? These questions often reveal an intra-generational divide within the Jewish community and also a difference in how Jews perceive themselves and how they are perceived by others. On the one hand, Jews are a tiny minority—they make up less than 2 percent of America's population and 0.2 percent of the world's. Our ancestors and immigrant predecessors often fled the scourge of antisemitism to arrive in new lands with very little to their names. Noble as the Jewish state's project of self-determination may be, it is born of a desperate need for a Jewish home—and this project is tested at every turn by hostile Arab neighbors. Synagogue attacks in Pittsburgh and Poway, and now October 7th—it is not hard to make the case that the Jewish people and state have been long and constantly embattled, and continue to be. We haven't imagined it.

And yet, by any measure—socially, economically, educationally, and politically, in both absolute and relative terms—it is a very good thing to be born a Jew today. The blessings enjoyed by American Jews, combined with the economic powerhouse and standing army of Israel—our predecessors could not have imagined this would be possible. Whatever our past (and sometimes present) sufferings, the comforts and achievements of American Jewry are formidable. In a curious and perhaps unprecedented state of affairs, contemporary Jewry can invoke both "underdog" and "overdog" status; we are persecuted and privileged at one and the same time, a fact of our existence important to name even if it lacks a tidy resolution.

A young person, who through no fault of their own holds Jewish points of reference based on Israel's strength and diaspora comforts, may be understandably mystified when the persecutions of the past are invoked. Similarly, the wider world, lacking a felt awareness of the centuries of homelessness and exile experienced by the Jews, may somewhat facilely conclude that the fact that Israel is surrounded by hostile Arab countries does not relieve it of its responsibilities to the suffering Palestinians in its midst. If anything, Jewish sufferings of the past should prompt Israel to "know the heart of the stranger" and treat its minority population as it would have wanted to be treated over millennia of exile. Given the considerable blessings of contemporary diaspora Jewry, in the eyes and ears of many, invocations of a persecuted past ring hollow. As became abundantly clear after October 7th, in a world governed by the spoken and unspoken rules of Diversity, Equity, and Inclusion (DEI), neither Jews nor Zionists are deemed to need any sort of protected status.

Are Jews guided by a universalizing empathy or a hardened vigilance? Are we powerless or powerful, outsiders or insiders, vulnerable or strong? We have been asking these questions for a very long time, arguably as far back as the events of the Passover story. They are part of the backstory of the Jewish experience, both diaspora and Israeli. They also help explain the kaleidoscope of responses in Israel, the diaspora, and around the world to the traumas of October 7th.

FIVE

ANTISEMITISM

A Modern Look at the World's Oldest Hate

Although I was born and raised in Los Angeles, my roots are British. My Manchester-born mother and Glasgow-born father arrived in America to pursue a job opportunity shortly before I was born, leaving their families. Around that same time, my mother's sister Leonie married my uncle David, a wonderful man from Leeds, England, where they settled down to raise seven children—six boys and a girl. Geography notwithstanding, the sisters remained close, a bond that continues to this day. Their children, the band of cousins of which I am one, always understood that but for the choices our parents made, our geographical location, accents, and lives could just have easily gone the other way. "I could be them and they could be me"—the unexpressed thought that bonds us together.

As a family committed to Judaism, my aunt and uncle sent their children to Jewish day school. Leeds, however, lacked a Jewish high school, so they decided that their children would make the two-hour commute each way, every day, to Manchester's King David High School. In the fall of

1994, four of them—Jonathan, Benji, Michael, and Rafi—took a trip to school that would change their lives forever.

Getting off the train in Manchester, they decided to walk the final blocks to school, passing a gangly group of seven men sitting on a railing off to the side. Not boys, not teenagers, but grown men began to follow them. Sensing that these men were no ordinary hooligans, my cousins picked up their pace, hoping to create some distance between them and their pursuers. Their King David school blazers identified them as Jewish.

The antisemitic slurs began. The thugs verbally taunted the oldest—Jonathan—while Benji, the second-oldest, tried to defuse the situation, hoping to pacify the men with gentle and no doubt self-deprecating humor. But the sharp words quickly turned into thrown rocks, and before Jonathan knew what was happening, he had been kicked in the back, then was head-butted at full force. The blow broke his nose and rendered him unconscious. The thugs, however, did not let Jonathan fall to the ground. They had other plans; their viciousness had only just begun. One held his limp body up so the others could hit and kick him.

Michael and Rafi, the little ones, ran frantically to the front doors of nearby homes, pleading for help. The residents opened their doors, poked their heads out to see what was going on, then shut the doors on the faces of my thirteen- and eleven-year-old cousins. Benji stood frozen at the sight of his older brother being beaten. Surely, he believed, at some point enough would be enough, the point had been made, the abuse would stop, and the bullies would move on.

Jonathan fell limp to the ground; unconscious, he was unable to curl his body into a protective fetal position as more rocks, bottles, and kicks flew at him. The ringleader of the gang shouted, "Kill the Jew!" Whatever naiveté or hope in humanity Benji held died at the moment. There would be no respite, no help forthcoming, no member of the gang saying "Enough is enough." Benji threw himself over his brother to absorb the blows—to be badly beaten himself.

The details of what happened next are fuzzy. My cousins recall the boots of the gang members being replaced by those of security guards from the train station, who finally arrived on the scene. Benji carried Jonathan the remaining blocks to the gate of the school, where the receptionist called for an ambulance. When my aunt, his mother, first saw Jonathan after he was brought home, his mangled condition shocked her; his face had been beaten beyond recognition.

The gang members, or at least some of them, were eventually apprehended. The price they paid for their crime was inconsequential: a fine of fifty pounds, rendered in installments over two years.

As for my cousins, their lives were changed forever. Jonathan has suffered from debilitating headaches and general poor health. The year following the attack, he was afflicted with cirrhosis of the liver—necessitating, over the years, four liver transplants. Now a practicing attorney in Leeds, Jonathan has courageously built a life for himself and created a beautiful family. His decision to stay in Leeds, however, was not entirely his own. Given the chronic ailments he has faced since that fateful day, he is, ironically, tethered to the health-care system of the city that inflicted upon him his health challenges in the first place.

My cousin Rafi, from that day forward, feared walking alone outside his house in the UK. A talented musician, he eventually immigrated to Israel, where he settled down and got married. My cousin Michael, now a promotional filmmaker in Brooklyn, developed alopecia soon after the attack, a condition of hair loss that has never interfered with his ability to be in the company of good-looking women. He has thankfully settled down and is the proud father of a little girl.

As for Benji, he spent the rest of high school going to the gym, where he learned how to box and defend himself. Never again, he vowed, would he let himself be pushed around. Benji too immigrated to Israel, serving on the front lines of the Second Lebanon War, and then Operation Pillar of Defense (2012), where his brother Rafi joined him in the infantry.

To this day, when I see my cousins, we share memories of our granny and poke fun at the quirks of the two sisters who are our mothers. In retrospect, that day became a defining pivot of self-understanding. The principles of their existence were upended; the hatred of others shaped who they would become, who they are today, and their sense of what it means to be a Jew in this world.

Uniformly bad, antisemitism is not uniform in expression. Over the course of its history, the world's oldest hatred has taken different forms. Not a single chapter of the book of Exodus goes by before Pharaoh gives expression to

a trope that would be repeated in different guises throughout history:

> Look, the Israelite people are too numerous for
> us. Let us deal shrewdly with them, so they may
> not increase; otherwise in the event of war they
> may join our enemies in fighting . . . So they [the
> Egyptians] set taskmasters over them to oppress
> them.
>
> *(Exodus 1:9–11)*

A people bearing ancestry and customs different from
those of the rest of the populace is identified. As they grow
in number, Pharaoh seeks to limit their power. He plays
off the unspoken fears of his people, portraying the Israelites as a threat, a fifth column capable of undermining
the nation from within, and he uses this to justify setting a
system of oppression in motion.

"History never repeats itself. Man always does," wrote
Voltaire (himself a perpetuator of negative stereotypes regarding Jews and Judaism). From the pyramids of Egypt
to the Purim story of ancient Persia, from the theologi-
cally fueled blood libels of Christian Europe to the hatreds
of Nazi ideology—as varied as the context and symptoms
may be, the pathology of the virus of antisemitism remains
the same. Difference transformed to fear, fear transformed
to hate, hate transformed to violence—whether state
sanctioned or not. The story has been repeated through
the ages.

Abundant as antisemitism has been throughout history,

so too is the literature about its origins, manifestations, and proposed cures. One helpful heuristic was offered by a founding leader of American Jewry as we enjoy it today, Solomon Schechter (1847–1915). The preeminent scholar of Jewish studies of his time, Schechter left his position at Cambridge University in 1902 to become president of the Jewish Theological Seminary of America (my alma mater)—a position he held with distinction until his death. To this day, Schechter's legacy continues to guide not just the institution he led, but by a certain telling, American Jewry as a whole.

Against the backdrop of surging expressions of antisemitism in Europe, in March 1903 Schechter delivered an address titled "Higher Criticism—Higher Anti-Semitism." In his remarks he coined a distinction between what he termed the lower antisemitism and the higher antisemitism.

Reflecting back on his Romanian youth, Schechter said that he would, much like my cousins, "come home from the Cheder [Hebrew school] bleeding and crying from the wounds inflicted upon [me] by the Christian boys." This was the "vulgar sort" of antisemitism, the lower kind. He included in his definition of this type of antisemitism his memories of his own bloodied childhood, the Hep Hep riots (a series of anti-Jewish pogroms that swept through Bavarian towns in 1819) and the trumped-up charges of treason leveled against Captain Alfred Dreyfus, a French Jew, in 1894. Just months after Schechter made these remarks, the previously noted anti-Jewish riots known as the Kishinev pogroms broke out; Schechter would have undoubtedly classified them as an expression of lower antisemitism—as he would the violence of October 7th.

The focus of Schechter's address, however, was not the physical suffering characterizing lower antisemitism, but rather the suffering inflicted by what he called "Higher Anti-Semitism." A pious Jew and man of the academy, Schechter called out scholars who employed what was then referred to as "higher criticism"—a form of biblical scholarship that, in brief, sought to identify the human rather than divine origins of the Hebrew Bible as understood by traditional Jews. A scholar of the highest rank, Schechter readily acknowledged many different findings of scholarly inquiry, but in "higher criticism" he detected antisemitism, in that it was an attempt to dethrone the Hebrew Bible from its sacred status—and, by extension, prove the spiritual essence of Judaism to be inferior.

Genteel and scholarly as the discourse of the academy may have been, for Schechter it was equally, if not more, nefarious than the thuggery of lower antisemitism. "Our great claim to the gratitude of mankind," Schechter said, "is that we gave to the world the word of God, the Bible." In Schechter's estimation, "the Bible is [the Jewish people's] sole raison d'être." Higher (biblical) criticism could be categorized as the higher antisemitism in that it was a venomous form of anti-Jewish scholarship. It denied Jews the sanctity of their religious texts and, by extension, the integrity of their faith.

∽

REMOVED AS SCHECHTER may be from our present time and circumstance, his language provides a scaffolding to speak about antisemitism. Jew hatred is neither monolithic nor, for that matter, is the study of it a precise science; its varied manifestations cannot be placed into tidy and discrete categories. It is, rather, a spectrum or sliding scale—from the most vulgar to the most genteel. At one end, acts of hate-filled violence, and at the other end, modest and sometimes barely perceptible sleight-of-hand exclusion, often, as in Schechter's day, cloaked in pseudo-scholarship.

Today, the lower antisemitism remains—violence against Jews because they are Jews: the murder of eleven Jewish souls at the Pittsburgh Tree of Life synagogue in 2018, the verbal bullying or physical brutality aimed at a Hasid in Brooklyn, and the antisemitic screeds in the dark and not-so-dark corners of the web. The shameless antisemitism emanating from the far right has included violent assaults and chants like those in Charlottesville: "Jews will not replace us." Lower antisemitism can come from the right or the left, from white nationalists or Islamic fundamentalists. The vicious attacks of October 7th were not just crimes against Israel, or humanity—they were assaults on Jewish lives. Sad to say, lower antisemitism is alive and well in our day.

Closely related to Schechter's lower form of antisemitism is what I would call a "middling" variety, which includes physical thuggery and also the power of words to do harm—vocal slurs, fear mongering, 9/11 conspiracy theorists' rants, intimidation of Jews on campus, hate and intimidation expressed online, rude graffiti, and the like. In such instances, one's physical person or property may not be violated but one's sense of self and safety is nonetheless compromised by a variety of anti-Jewish hate mongering: graffiti, slurs, online hate and intimidation, and much more.

The International Holocaust Remembrance Alliance (IHRA) defines antisemitism as "a certain perception of Jews, which may be expressed as hatred toward Jews. Rhetorical and physical manifestations of antisemitism directed toward Jewish or non-Jewish individuals and/or their property, toward Jewish community institutions and religious facilities." Tracked by institutions like the ADL, kept to a low burn in law-abiding societies, middling antisemitism has of late had an uptick, shown in anti-Israel rhetoric intended to intimidate all Jews, as well as the verbal and physical confrontations taking place in our country and across the internet.

Identifiable as the "lower" and "middle" antisemitisms may be, it is the higher antisemitism that is arguably most widespread, difficult to discern, and thus most pernicious. In Schechter's time, the proxy for hatred was the Jew's claim on a sacred text—the Bible. Today it is the Jew's claim to a sacred land, Israel, and by extension, the Jewish right to self-determination and self-defense, which is the proxy for contemporary antisemitism. Were Schechter to write today, he would write: "Our [the Jewish people's] great claim to the gratitude of mankind is that we gave to the world . . . Israel." Often, what people are saying about Israel is really what they're saying about Jews.

To be sure, we could make the case that the blurring of lines between criticism of Israel and criticism of Jews is fair game. I pray on behalf of the Jewish state, and the flag of the modern State of Israel sits proudly on the pulpit of my synagogue; I devote an extraordinary amount of my rabbinate to ensuring the well-being of Israel. I readily admit that my Jewish identity and my Zionism are inseparable, the latter wholly emergent from the former. If this is so, why should I be offended or even surprised if non-Jews conflate discussions and criticisms of Israel with criticisms of the Jewish community?

Moreover, as someone who has publicly and privately critiqued Israel, its leadership, its Chief Rabbinate, its inability to house religious pluralism, its inability to realize the ideals of its founding declaration to be a Jewish and democratic state, I fully believe that my criticism is an expression of my love for Israel and Judaism. So too, there have been and continue to be non-Zionist expressions of Jewish life. Misguided and shortsighted as I believe non-statist formulations of contemporary Jewish life to be, they are not in and of themselves antisemitic. I do not begrudge the critics of Israel their right to criticism.

And yet it is an inescapable reality that embedded in anti-Zionism are not-so-hidden expressions of antisemitism. Sometimes they are easy to detect. The use of the prefix "Zio" ("Zio-media," "Zio-economics," and so on) can cloak hatred of Jews. The left wing's critique of Zionism as a colonial project born of sin ignores the thousands of years of Jewish claim to the land, the present-day case for a Jewish nation-state, and cycle after cycle of Arab rejectionism of any Jewish presence in the Middle East. The word *Zionist* itself is a convenient and fungible term used by antisemites to mask Jew hatred. To the contemporary antisemite, Zionism has become the equivalent of the blood libels of old. Here are a people, they are different from us, this difference gives life to a fear that they will grow too numerous and powerful. It follows the pattern of hatred first expressed in Exodus.

WHILE THE INCREASED threat of the lower and middle antisemitisms would be enough to raise alarm bells for Jews, the increase in the third, higher antisemitism has, I believe, stung the most and shaken American Jewry to its core. All the woke justifications, moral equivalencies, "yeah buts," and whataboutisms that arose after October 7th have led to the unnerving realization that perhaps Jews are not quite as secure in America as we had thought we were. This threat is not the exact equivalent of an attack against Israelis, or a horrific shooting by a lunatic-fringe white nationalist, or the disturbed rantings of an NBA point guard or unhinged rapper. We recognize something less physically violent but more nefarious: that in the eyes of many, Jewish lives are worth less than other lives.

This is happening right here on our own front yard, in the institutions we are part of, in our friends' posts on Facebook, on the boards we sit on, and in organizations that some of us fund. We connect the dots from an antisemitic conference on a campus to the upended tables at a Hillel House, from the silence of a school administration in the face of the loss of Jewish life to the bullying of a Jewish student. We experience moral whiplash when, after Israeli Jews have been murdered or kept in continuing captivity, we hear voices in our society claim that the violence is justified. It's as if a curtain has been ripped away, revealing an unexpected reality and leaving us to wonder where we, as Jews, fit in.

Not too long ago, I brought a group of synagogue teens to Berlin, a capstone experience for our bright soon-to-be graduates of high school. We went to learn about our synagogue's German Jewish heritage, interact with German Jews, and, most of all, learn about the origins of our people's darkest hour—the Holocaust. Having visited Auschwitz, Theresienstadt, and other concentration camps with other groups, I believed, and in many respects still do, that I had already visited a few of the sites of the worst atrocities committed against Jews and all of humanity. The train tracks, the barracks, the selection lines, the crematoria—a window onto the evil that humans are capable of perpetrating against one another.

It was, nonetheless, a disturbing experience of an altogether different kind to visit the Wannsee Conference Center in an idyllic suburb twenty minutes outside Berlin. It was in this lakeside conference resort that fifteen high-ranking officials met on January 20, 1942, to coordinate the implementation of the "Final Solution." With beautiful views, elegant waitstaff, and bureaucratic efficiency, the highly credentialed officials formalized a plan of genocide against the Jews; without them, the machinery of the death camps would have never been set in motion. Millions of European Jews were murdered in the death camps, but their death warrants were signed long before—before the train tracks, before even Wannsee. Their noose was prepared by way of hundreds of previous acts of dehumanization and exclusion. Excluded from professions, from participating in civic society, they were deemed other, regarded as a threat, made less than human, making their mass murder seem far more mundane than would have been otherwise possible.

My point is decidedly not that the genocide of Jews is around the corner. It's important to be cautious when drawing historical analogies. I make the more modest but critically important point that the movement from the higher forms of antisemitism to the lower forms can happen easily, imperceptibly, and quickly. The thugs who beat up my cousins no doubt harbored hatreds instilled in them long before they spotted the four visibly Jewish brothers on their way to school.

The perpetrators of those acts, and any hate-based act of violence, have moral agency. And yet without a series of seeders, enablers, and bystanders, the violent acts themselves would not be committed. The institutions molding identity, be it media, schools, houses of worship, or individual homes, all contribute to the shaping of the character of a given society. Political extremism, toxic discourse, and social media are the enablers. Most damning are the bystanders who, at every stage of antisemitism's continuum of hate, fail to stand up and put a halt before a further stage can be reached. From the highest of highs to the lowest of lows—intellectual hatreds lead to violent expression of hatreds. As the German poet Heinrich Heine famously wrote, "Those who burn books will in the end burn people."

The progression from one form of antisemitism to the next, then to the next, and so on, is not a necessary one. As the ad on the New York subways reminds us: "If you see something, say something." Or maybe better yet—do something. From the right, the left, or the higher, middle, or lower, antisemitism must be called out, confronted, and quashed. Not just Jews but all people of conscience should not tolerate baseless hatreds of any kind.

As I grapple to understand where and who we are as Jews today, my thoughts inevitably turn to that day so many years ago in provincial England. I think of my cousins called upon, time and again, to defend themselves and their Jewish heritage. I think of the day when they—yiddische boys in their school blazers—banged in vain on neighborhood doors, crying for help. Never again would they allow their safety and that of their brothers to be dependent on the kindness of strangers. Never again would a naive belief in the goodness of humanity lead them to hesitate in fulfilling their obligations to defend themselves as their attackers prepared their assault. It would be their decision—theirs and their country's alone—to choose the moment and manner by which their destiny would be shaped and their safety secured. They remain the same cousins, the world has changed, and yet antisemitism, the world's oldest hatred, remains and continues to shape-shift and proliferate. Who would have believed that on October 7th, and over the months that followed, we would see this hatred, in all its manifestations, emerge with ferocity, diversity, and ubiquity, as it did? My cousins, I must believe, were not surprised. Why were we?

PART TWO

What Is

SIX

GRIEF, CLARITY, SOLIDARITY

Anchors for This Moment in Time

The day that Israel was suddenly and viciously attacked by Hamas terrorists—October 7, 2023—is a date, like December 7, 1941, and September 11, 2001, that will live in infamy. Over 1,100 murdered, over 3,000 wounded, and over 240 men, women, children, babies, and seniors taken hostage. Women raped, families bound and burned alive, and parents and children forced to witness one another's murder. As of this writing, more than 130 souls are still held hostage in Gaza, where they have been captive for more than six months.

So many emotions, so many questions. Who had been killed? Who had been captured? What was the fate of the hostages? How did Israel not see this coming? How had they been so badly caught off guard? Would Israel's northern border with Hezbollah be the next front of war? Would the Palestinian community inside Israel and the West Bank erupt in violence? Would this first attack be seen as an opportunity for Israel's enemies—Iran's proxies and others—to pounce? October 7th was not spontaneous: the events of that day reflected careful, long-term planning. What else was being planned?

I understood that this was a leadership moment—that I would need to say something to my community. But what? I had no idea. Shockingly, in the days that followed the attack, much of public opinion began to turn against Israel; though victimized, Israel was already being portrayed as an aggressor. In the week that followed the attacks, anti-Israel rallies sprouted up across the United States; incredibly, the participants voiced solidarity with Hamas.

Hamas and its allies declared that Friday, the first Shabbat following the attacks, a Global Day of Rage, with social media posts bearing instructions to "attack Israelis and Jews." Shabbat is when we gather as a congregation, and the security concerns for my community—a large, public-facing urban synagogue—were not inconsequential. As I was wondering what to say to my congregants, I knew that many of them were understandably wondering whether it was safe to enter the synagogue at all.

"Stay in your lane," I remember counseling myself. "You are neither a political scientist nor a military strategist. You are a rabbi, a pastor to your flock, and preacher and teacher of sacred texts."

In its purest expression, the rabbinic vocation is a calling to interpret sacred Jewish texts through the prism of personality in a manner that speaks to the needs of the day. This was a time to get back to basics. I decided to ask myself the same three questions I ask whenever I sit down to write a sermon: What is the scriptural reading of the week, how does it speak to this moment, and what message does my community need to hear?

Over the course of the services on Friday night and Saturday morning, I preached from three texts from that Shabbat's Torah reading—the opening chapters of the book of Genesis. On that day, and every day since, those three texts have informed how I view the events of October 7th. As we move further from the attacks, they speak with increasing urgency.

GRIEF

And God created humankind in the
divine image, in the image of God,
God created humanity.

(GENESIS 1:27)

This verse from the first chapter of Genesis roots the primordial origins of our species and holds unique primacy in biblical theology. The creation of humanity in God's image—in Hebrew, *tzelem elohim*, reflects far more than a comment on the human figure—that our physical features somehow reflect the divine form. Throughout the ages, the verse has come to be understood to speak to humanity's shared spiritual essence—namely, that every human being is created with an element or, as the mystics would say, a spark of the divine.

Long before October 7th, this verse has been the foundational building block of my theology. Every human being—male, female, or nonbinary, old and young and in between, straight and gay, rich and poor, believer and nonbeliever—is created equally in God's image. No matter one's race, religion, or nationality, regardless of whether a person is a friend or foe—they are created in the image of God. As such, they are to be accorded equal and infinite dignity as befitting God's creation. Insofar as a religious life can be understood as the quest for the divine, *tzelem elohim* reminds us that this quest is pursued not only by way of prayerful petitions to the heavens. A religious life is also constituted by a lifetime of inquiries into the condition of other human souls—inquiries aimed at identifying, nurturing, and protecting the divine spark embedded in every fellow creation. The rabbis of old teach that humanity, created as we are in the image of God, is endowed with the ability to "be godly" in our actions—in Latin, *imitatio Dei*. By performing acts of kindness (visiting the sick, feeding the hungry, clothing the poor), we imitate God's compassionate ways—junior partners, if you will, in completing God's creation.

Why begin here? Because October 7th was a violation of first principles—God's image had been desecrated. My heart was broken, presumably God's too, and that sorrow needed to be named.

The murders of that day? One would have been too many. As the Talmud teaches, "Whosoever destroys a single soul, it is as if they have destroyed an entire universe." The attacks were a vile crime perpetrated against innocents, the very foundations of our faith, and the underlying bond of our common humanity.

In the days and weeks that followed, the brutal inhumanity of Hamas's attacks would emerge. A hall of horrors, filled with premediated acts of sheer savagery. Charred wrists bearing marks of individuals' hands bound behind their backs before they were burned alive—the soot in the trachea revealing that they were still living when immolated. The remains of two individuals—one adult, one child—showed that they had been tied together by metal wire before they were set aflame. Evidence of countless horrific crimes of sexual violence. Rape, bodily mutilation, and the two occurring simultaneously.

The facts are damning and indisputable—based on firsthand testimony and incontestable forensic evidence. Unlike other instances of war crimes, in which the perpetrators managed to deny or cover up the atrocities they committed, no such obstacles to investigation were encountered. Indeed, the strongest testimony came from the perpetrators themselves, who, by way of their phones and GoPro body cameras, documented their deeds, celebrated them, uploaded them to their social media accounts, and called home to their beaming parents to tell them of the gruesome deeds they had committed that day. "Look how many I killed with my own hands! Your son killed Jews!" relayed one Hamas terrorist in a recorded call to his parents. "I wish I was with you," the mother replied. No matter one's faith, political leanings, or connection to the Middle East, look and you will see that this was the face of evil, revealed and unleashed in our lifetime.

It was and is too much to bear. The vicious murders, the heart-wrenching grief of the family members who escaped harm, the lifetime of trauma in store for the survivors, the ongoing nightmare of the hostages and their families.

Every victim—a unique contribution to creation, a spark of the divine—had been violently snuffed out.

As we read the profiles of the victims, the tragedy was compounded and given texture. Many were idealistic kibbutzniks—from Israel's peace camp—some had been deeply invested in Palestinian-Israeli coexistence, people who, prior to October 7th, would help transport Gazans to Israeli hospitals for medical care. Young men and women attending a music festival—364 murdered in a single location. The victims robbed of their lives and their dreams; their shattered loved ones staring at a lifetime of loss and sorrow.

As a rabbi who has shepherded countless families through loss, I understood that my first task at hand was a pastoral one—to help a community grieve a devastating blow. The sorrows of the moment were overwhelming— some congregants were less than a few degrees of separation from the victims and their families. For those who weren't, it was nevertheless a profound blow to the global Jewish family. The victims were members of the human family, but within my community they were members of the Jewish family; in Hebrew, my *mishpacha*. There was, and remains, a palpable sense that Israelis were not murdered that day, but rather Jews. I recall seeing a colleague at a rally the week after the assaults, who shared that he wished he could wake up from this nightmare. I responded that I only wished I could fall asleep. In the years to come, I have no doubt that studies will show how deeply our patterns of sleeping, eating, intimacy, and more were impacted by the events of that day.

That first Friday night service following the attack began with the feeling of a funeral—or at least a memorial service. Indeed, in the wake of October 7th, I was reminded of the wisdom of the ritualized phases of Jewish mourning, the one week (shiva), the thirty days (shloshim), and the year (kaddish); phases that track, more or less, the stages of grief associated with loss—shock, sorrow, acceptance. In my years serving families through loss, I have learned that no rabbi can remove a person's grief—it is an emotion we manage but never transcend. Often the role of the rabbi is merely (but importantly) to "name" the moment for what it is, with the hope that the mourner will sense that what they are experiencing is normal, that they are not alone, that although no two people experience loss alike, others are walking through that same valley of the shadow of death.

God's creation, members of our extended Jewish family, had been killed. Our grief needed to be given a name, an emotional scaffolding and community of support. We needed to be reminded what had been lost, the divine spark of so many that had been snuffed out.

CLARITY

Cain said to Abel his brother . . . and when
they were in the field, Cain set upon
his brother Abel and killed him.

(GENESIS 4:8)

The crowning glory of the first chapter of Genesis is the creation of humanity in the image of God; the shedding of human blood that follows shortly thereafter reveals the depths to which humanity can sink. This second text, the first instance of biblical fratricide, serves as a scriptural backdrop for contending with the pernicious moral equivalencies that emerged in the wake of the attacks of October 7th.

Born to Adam and Eve following their departure from the Garden of Eden, the first brothers of human history have a famously fraught relationship. Cain is a tiller of soil, and Abel a sheepherder. Each brother makes an offering to God, but for reasons that are never made clear, God pays no heed to Cain's offering. Downcast and distressed, Cain refuses to be consoled by God, understandably so, given that God's earlier rejection of his offering is the root of his frustration.

Genesis 4:8 is the key verse, and its significance is not immediately self-evident. It requires a bit of explanation. The text is not just laconic in style, but awkwardly incomplete. It reads: "Va-yomer kayin el hevel . . . vay'hi b'heyotam ba-sadeh." ("And Cain said to Abel . . . and when they were in the field, Cain set upon his brother and killed him.") It is clear that the brothers speak to each other, and it is clear that once in the field, Cain kills his brother. What is not clear, and what is never stated, is what Cain says to Abel. The lacuna is part of the text itself. There is no biblical record of the exchange that prompted Cain to rise up and kill his brother.

Interpreters through the ages have made much about the missing text. This is, after all, the Bible, a holy book not imagined as susceptible to typos, editorial slips, and verses poorly stitched together. The Septuagint, the Greek translation of the Bible, fills in the gap with this dialogue:

"Come let us go to the field." Other ancient translations do the same. Some later rabbinic commentators imagine an exchange filled with enmity; others, fraternal jealousy. Still others suggest that a dispute erupts between the brothers over their inheritance from their parents. There are as many explanations as there are interpreters.

I can understand the impulse to fill the textual gap and in so doing provide a context for Cain's heinous deed—but with all due respect to my rabbinic predecessors, I think that they all have it wrong.

The fragmented nature of the text is altogether intentional; the ellipsis within it is its very point. There is nothing that could have happened, nothing that could have been said to justify Cain's murder of his brother. In leaving the dialogue unstated, the Bible provides moral clarity. It is not about context, no dueling "he said / he said," no misunderstanding that could justify Abel's murder, that he somehow "had it coming." Nothing can justify Cain's criminal act of aggression, so the Torah refrains from doing so. This message is consistent with that of an earlier biblical scene, the eating of the fruit of the garden in which humanity is endowed with the Godlike ability to differentiate between good and evil. Indeed, if there is a point to these first chapters of the Torah (Garden of Eden, Tower of Babel, Noah's Ark), it is to remind us that we have agency over our decisions. There is right and there is wrong, and no context or circumstance can justify Cain's murderous deeds.

If the first task of rabbinic leadership in our post–October 7th reality was to name the sorrow and provide comfort in the face of tragic loss, then the second was to provide moral clarity. By a certain telling, this is the underlying reason why people turn to religion. When our world becomes untethered, we turn to faith, scripture, and tradition for stability. October 7th unleashed unspeakable evil: an ideology that would kill Jews for being Jews and commit murder for sport. This ideology represents neither the Muslim faith, the national interests of the Palestinian people, nor any vision of future coexistence between Palestinians and Israelis. Rape is not a form of protest. Killing babies is not an expression of conscience. Taking hostages is not the tool of a freedom fighter. There is no justification, no moral equivalency, nothing that could satisfactorily contextualize the murderous crimes committed by Hamas on October 7th. Evil is evil.

The community I serve is fairly centrist in its politics regarding the Palestinian-Israeli conflict. Notwithstanding outliers on the far left and far right, generally speaking, my synagogue's love for Israel carries with it commitment to a vision of peaceful coexistence between Israelis and Palestinians. Jews were once strangers in a strange land. How could Israel, a state with a Jewish majority, not be sympathetic to the rights of the minority in its midst? How could Israel fight for its own right to self-determination and deny Palestinians access to that same right?

Palestinian self-determination is considered a practical matter to most members of my community. The thinking goes like this: Isn't a Palestinian homeland the best way to ensure Israel's security? Let them enjoy all the opportunities and headaches of sovereignty, and let everyone get on with their lives. It is not a perfect solution, nor for that matter does it exculpate either side of its responsibility for the heartbreaking conflict—but it is the only path forward. We may quibble over the status of the borders, the timing of any such agreement, and the precise nature of Palestinian self-determination (statehood, self-rule, autonomy), but the general outline is there to see, and as non-voting, non-military-serving, non-tax-paying diaspora stakeholders in Israel's well-being, we acknowledge that the particulars are best left to Israelis and Palestinians to work out.

As textured and balanced as my inner dialogue (in my community and in my own head) may be, as committed as I am to interrogating my own views, the events of October 7th do not permit any such nuance. No historical land dispute, no he said / she said debate over competing narratives as to how we arrived at this point, is conscionable in the face of an ideology of violence aimed at my people to destroy them. As the late Israeli author and champion of Israel's political left Amos Oz once reflected: "One cannot approach Hamas and say: 'Maybe we meet halfway, and Israel only exists on Mondays, Wednesdays, and Fridays.'" The charter of Hamas is unambiguous in its call for the destruction for the Jewish state. October 7th revealed its intentions in full, bringing to mind Maya Angelou's comment: "When people show you who they are, believe them the first time." Much as we seek and pray for the prophetic day when swords will be turned into plowshares, Israel has every right to defend itself against those who seek its destruction.

In that first post–October 7th Shabbat, I was compelled to note the atrocities and to name the evil, because I knew what was coming next. I knew to expect the usual traffickers in online hate. Even the anti-Jewish hatred of the intelligentsia—like the Cornell University professor who described the actions of Hamas as "exhilarating"—though shocking was not surprising. But naively, I didn't imagine that the brutal facts of the day would need to be stated again and again. How could the rationale behind the atrocities be denied when their perpetrators celebrated them and expressed their intent to repeat similar actions until Israel is destroyed?

And yet, this is exactly what happened—from online platforms to the streets, from the statements of conspiracy theorists to the campus debates denying, minimizing, or contextualizing the events of October 7th and every subsequent action Israel took in self-defense. As the US ambassador Deborah Lipstadt noted: "The speed at which denialism has spread since October 7th is unprecedented." Akin to the Holocaust denier, who seeks to undercut the argument for the Jewish people's need for self-determination, those who airbrushed the atrocities of October 7th cast Israel's efforts to secure its defense, root out Hamas, and return the hostages as an indefensible act of aggression—a war of obligation reframed as a war of choice. Lest we forget, because hostages were taken, the atrocities of October 7th were not limited to October 7th. Every day that every hostage remains in captivity is an additional terror attack of sorts.

One of the most shocking aspects of the rhetoric of Israel's detractors, who decry what seems to them an out-of-proportion response to the crisis, is that they do not extend their righteous indignation to the suffering of the hostages by demanding their release. Such a move would be in accord with international law (article 34 of the Geneva conventions), and if accomplished, it would fundamentally change Israel's justifications for prosecuting a war. But in the months following October 7th, the plight of the hostages was not front and center in the eyes of progressives, revealing that hatred for Israel, not love for progressive principles or respect for international law, fueled their efforts.

"From time to time, evils appear on the world scene which are in a class unto themselves . . . ," wrote the late political philosopher Michael Wyschogrod. Horrific as the events of October 7th were, for a fleeting moment they provided moral clarity. As Jews, not only do we believe that such evil can exist in this world, but we have a word for it, and that word is Amalek.

"Remember what Amalek did to you as you came forth out of Egypt; how he met you on the way, and cut down all the stragglers at your rear, when you were faint and weary" (Deuteronomy 25:17–19). When the Israelites left Egypt for the Promised Land, they had scarcely crossed the sea when Amalek attacked. In the biblical and rabbinic tradition, the pedigrees of those who have persecuted Israel—Agag, Haman, Rome, and others—are all traced back to Amalek. The enemies of the Jewish people are not one and the same—the Roman Empire is not Khmelnitzky, the Iranians are not the Nazis, Haman is not Hamas—it is both inaccurate and unhelpful to draw the analogy too close. But what these disparate ideologies have in common is the Amalek belief that Jews should not achieve the thing every person and every nation wants: safety and self-determination.

"In the face of abnormal evil, abnormal responses are necessary," writes Wyschogrod. "There comes a point when military intervention is justified, and the religious community has a duty to speak clearly when that point is reached." In Hamas, our generation is confronting Amalek's latest incarnation. An Israeli response is both justified and necessary. It is precisely because Jews in Israel today, unlike those of bygone days, have a standing army to defend themselves that the threat of Amalek can be confronted. As Amos Oz reminded us, in 1945 the lives of those in Theresienstadt were saved not by peace demonstrators with placards and flowers but by soldiers and submachine guns.

In the months since October 7th, Israel has engaged in a terrifying war with Hamas. Its campaign to root out Hamas (often situated in hospitals and civilian populations), free the hostages, and secure Israel from future attacks is justified, but it has come at a terrible human cost. As of this writing, tens of thousands of Palestinians have been killed, even more injured, and millions displaced and suffering unimaginable hunger. This humanitarian crisis and human tragedy is beyond comprehension. Yet as excruciating as the questions surrounding it may be, it is altogether reasonable to ask about the human cost of Israel's campaign. To do otherwise is to lack compassion for a suffering humanity. It is also why, whenever I speak about the war, without fail I mention October 7th and the ongoing plight of the hostages. In the face of the tsunami of denialism and disinformation, it is not much. But to those who are listening, it is a reminder of the moral footing upon which we stand.

SOLIDARITY

The third biblical verse that has been ever-present in my mind since the attacks is Genesis 4:9: "The Lord said to Cain, 'Where is your brother Abel?' And he said, 'I do not know. Am I my brother's keeper?'"

I preached from this text on that fateful Shabbat, and it continues to guide my response to the attacks of October 7th. The verse comes immediately following the previously quoted one about the murder itself. Cain has killed Abel, and not a verse passes before his deed is discovered. As was the case when God called out for Adam and Eve following their eating of the hidden fruit, God's question to Cain regarding Abel's whereabouts is not just about location. God knows exactly where Abel is and what Cain has done. In Genesis 4:10, the following verse, God offers an evocative rejoinder: "The sound of your brother's blood cries from the ground."

Cain's missteps are manifold—his inability to master his impulses, the murder itself, and the shoulder-shrug lie regarding the whereabouts of his brother's body. The sin for which he is most remembered is his impertinent retort: "Am I my brother's keeper?" There is much to be said about Cain's response. His evasiveness, his denial of moral responsibility, his chutzpah before God even as he acknowledges his fraternal bond.

Whatever thought motivated his response—he got the

answer wrong. "Thou shalt not stand idly by your fellow's blood," we read later in the Torah (Leviticus 19:16). The moral exemplars of our tradition take a tack opposite to Cain's. Abraham pleads before God on behalf of Sodom, a city of wickedness. Moses, while still living in the household of Pharaoh, witnesses an Egyptian taskmaster beating his Hebrew kinsman. "And he looked this way and that way and saw no person, and he struck down the Egyptian" (Exodus 2:12). In a moment when nobody was stepping up—Moses stepped up to save a life. In this scene Moses proves himself worthy of leading the people out of Egypt. By such a telling, we are measured according to our willingness to refuse to be a bystander—always, and especially, when the blood of one's brother cries out from the earth. This is the test that Cain fails. A teacher of mine once said that the entire system of Jewish ethics may be viewed as a response to Cain's impertinent question. Yes—we are our brother's and sister's keeper. It is the backbone to who we are.

That first Shabbat after the attacks, I called on my community to step up to the calling of the hour. We would not stand by as the blood of our brothers and sisters was shed. Unlike Hamas, our response would not be days of rage, but days of *ḥesed*—the Hebrew word for kindness and advocacy on behalf of our kinsmen.

I reminded my community of an earlier chapter in Israel's history, a story told to me by my father in 1967 when, with the outbreak of the Six-Day War, Israel's fate hung in the balance. The chief rabbi of the United Kingdom at that time, Rabbi Immanuel Jakobovits, called for a massive rally at London's Royal Albert Hall. Thousands turned out.

My father, a newly minted physician, was present there that day. The chief rabbi demanded that everyone do something, one of three things, he said. First: If one could go to Israel, go. Help Israel defend itself. My father was one of the many volunteers who spent that summer in Israel's hospitals, tending to the wounded. Second: If you can't go, then look after the interests of a person who is going. *Kol Yisrael arevim zeh ba-zeh*: "All of Israel is responsible for one another," as stated in the Talmud. Make sure their business or job or place in school is there upon their return. Third: If you are not positioned to do the first or the second thing, then give. Give money to support those who are positioned to save Jewish lives under threat. Every person has an obligation, by the bonds of Jewish history and Jewish peoplehood, to stem Jewish suffering in this dark hour.

That was 1967. This was 2023.

On the day of attacks, UJA Federation, New York's primary Jewish social service agency, established a fund specifically to provide relief to the hard-hit communities in Israel. My synagogue decided to print QR codes, to distribute in person and on the livestream feed for those watching from afar, which would send potential donors to the site where they could contribute. Unorthodox as it is to raise money on the Sabbath, I believed, and continue to believe, that in breaking the laws of Sabbath I was serving the higher law of saving a life (in Hebrew, *pikuach nefesh*). When I told everyone to take out their phones to do some fundraising, my daughter, who was in the pews that night, gasped audibly. To see her father raise funds on Shabbat? This was new territory. I explained to my community that when God calls me to account for my breach of Sabbath law, I will stand tall at the gates of heaven with questions of my own regarding the deaths of innocents in the week gone by. Prepared as I was for blowback from my rabbinic colleagues for fundraising on the Shabbat, the feedback I would receive in the days that followed was otherwise. Reform, Conservative, and Orthodox rabbis of stature reached out to me thanking me for my leadership.

My goal was $18 million—according to Jewish numerology, the number 18 corresponds to the Hebrew word *chai,* meaning life. I remember two things about announcing the goal to the full sanctuary. First, a silence punctuated by someone's awkward giggle of disbelief. "Who does this guy think he is, citing that number?" I imagined that person thinking. And then, I continued. "I am not unprepared. We are already sixteen million in." And the room broke out in applause.

What I hadn't shared before that moment was what I had done over the past week. I had spent every waking hour calling every philanthropically minded congregant I knew of, to ask them to contribute. Every dollar raised was going to Israel's relief. As a congregational rabbi, I spend a good deal of my time raising funds needed to keep the synagogue afloat, and Park Avenue isn't just any synagogue. The names of some of its members can be found on hospitals, institutions of higher learning, and charities of every variety. I admit that I wondered if it was for exactly a moment like this—for such a time as this—that I had become rabbi of Park Avenue Synagogue: to mobilize my congregation on behalf of the Jewish people. The pace was frenetic. When I felt tired, I thought of the lives lost, the hostages whose fate was unknown, and the IDF soldiers on the front lines. They were, in retrospect, the most profound and no-nonsense fundraising calls I have ever made.

Not one person said no. By early the following week, I received a call from Lori, the fundraising professional at UJA. We had blown past the goal of $18 million. Should we announce the actual total we had raised? For two reasons we agreed not to. First, as any fundraiser knows, a campaign is never "closed"; one never announces that a goal has been reached—more support is always needed. Second, we both understood that, as proud as we were of our efforts, the funds we had raised were just a drop in the bucket. The news coming out of Israel was getting worse and worse. Billions, not millions, were needed to address Israel's needs.

Philanthropy was and remains the primary means by which my community or any diaspora community can help alleviate a crisis on the other side of the world. Most gratifying was the grassroots spirit that energized the community. Bake sales, collection drives, educational initiatives. One resourceful parent baked challahs, selling her wares week in and week out. Another three mothers proclaimed themselves "Yisrael Yentas" and set in motion a slew of initiatives. Many congregants began to mobilize politically, hosting and attending events in favor of officials and would-be officials who supported Israel's right to self-defense and self-determination. We began to wear dog-tag "Bring Them Home" necklaces—reminders to ourselves and everyone we met of the plight of the hostages. We wrote letters and attended rallies in New York and Washington, DC. In the months following October 7th, our congregants stepped up to advocate on behalf of Israel in the public sphere. Our congregation offered two solidarity and volunteer missions to Israel; each one sold out within hours.

As I've repeatedly said to the community, "We are traumatized, but we are not paralyzed." Announcing to the world that we are indeed our brother's keeper, our community rose up in more ways than can be counted or will ever be known.

Months have passed, and much has transpired since October 7th. We live day by day with the plight of the hostages, the death toll of the Palestinians, the fallen and wounded Israeli soldiers, and the ever-changing global response. Yet no matter the distance traveled, my moral compass continues to point to the grief that resulted from the attacks themselves, which left an indelible scar on the soul and psyche of the Jewish people. I also stay focused on the right of Israel to defend itself in the face of an enemy that would see it destroyed. The obligation to stand in solidarity with our brothers and sisters in their hour of need has not diminished.

In the face of a world turned upside down, I am steadied by the texts of our tradition that provide solace and guidance. Ancient as our sacred texts may be, with every passing day they speak with an urgency to me, to the community I serve, and to the ever-evolving landscape of our post–October 7th world.

SEVEN

THE TRIBAL MOMENT

What It Means to Be Jewish Today

Shortly after the October 7th attacks, my third daughter, Zoe, returned home from campus for her fall break.

"Dad," she announced at the dinner table. "Do you know what the difference is between COVID and October 7th?"

"What?" I replied.

"During COVID none of us were physically where we wanted to be—at camp, at school, at work, wherever. We were physically displaced. But it was a global pandemic; it wasn't personal; everyone was equally affected—we were emotionally 'in place.'

"October 7th," she continued, "is different. Physically we are all pretty much 'in place'; we're on campus, living our lives; we are where we are supposed to be. The problem is that emotionally we are all 'displaced.' None of us knows where we stand."

I was struck by my daughter's observation—its insight and vulnerability. It describes how many American Jews of all ages feel after October 7th. We have lost our emotional coordinates and mooring.

It has been a time of deep loneliness for Jews. Like a

mourner who, upon losing a loved one, reenters society and yet feels disoriented when others do not share their grief—so it is for Jews in the post–October 7th world. It is hard to participate in cultural touchpoints—to watch sports, go to movies or concerts—knowing what is going on in Israel and Gaza. The watercooler chitchat that typically punctuates our work environment rings false, even seems to be in bad taste. For a time the streets of New York were canvased with photos of the hostages. As we passed them, my wife would "tap and kiss" each one—as a religious Jew would "kiss" a mezuzah on the lintel of a doorpost. Often, the signs (on the streets and on social media feeds) reflect the "other" side—at best ignoring the events of October 7th, at worst blaming the attacks on Israel. Wait—weren't we the victims? Sometimes it feels like the world has lost its moral compass. We feel incredulity, disbelief, and yes—deep loneliness.

But we have also experienced something beautiful and uniting: a tribal awakening. Our feelings of vulnerability are intermixed with solidarity, our disillusionment with moral clarity. There is a sharpening of our sense of kinship, the feeling that indeed, we are a people who dwell apart. It is a time of profound pain and disorientation, but it also carries with it a sense of discovery and a quickening to this existential moment. Even in our dark hour, we are searching and often finding a deep, abiding connection to our community, our culture, and our faith. Fear and courage. Helplessness and a sense of duty to our people. Untethered and yet more connected than ever.

Not just in public acts of solidarity but in quiet acts of

Jewish inquiry and exploration, I can track an "awakening" of Jewish identity. Shortly after the attacks, the mother of an early childhood student in my synagogue came to see me. After some preliminary small talk, she confessed that while she was raised Jewish and always identified as being Jewish—given that her mother's mother was "technically" not Jewish, she knew that by certain definitions she was not considered Jewish according to Jewish law. It was a quirk in her identity that never bothered her—until October 7th. What steps would be needed, she asked me, to "complete" her Jewish identity? In the weeks to come, we scheduled a visit to the mikveh—the water immersion that, according to Jewish law, would "complete" her Jewish identity.

Another example: For some time, I had been working with an adorable young interfaith couple who, for their own reasons, were not on the fast track for the non-Jewish woman to convert to Judaism or, for that matter, to get married. Sometime after October 7th, they came to my office to talk. Given the attacks, the young man wondered whether his girlfriend should still convert; after all, if things got really bad for the Jews, he would be safer married to a non-Jew. After he voiced this thinking, she responded with the opposite view, insisting that it was precisely at such a time as this that she *must* convert and tie her destiny to the Jewish people. Truth be told, I have not completely made sense of all that was said in my office that day. I do know that she has since converted, and a wedding date is in the works. Loneliness and solidarity—mixed together to make a tribal awakening.

I have found it helpful to understand the significance of

our tribal moment by way of a distinction between what my colleague and friend Rabbi Donniel Hartman calls "Genesis Jews," and "Exodus Jews." Despite their proximity in the biblical canon, Genesis and Exodus, the first two books of the Hebrew bible, read as very different texts. Genesis relates the family stories of our biblical matriarchs and patriarchs—Sarah, Rebecca, Rachel, and Leah; Abraham, Isaac, Jacob, and Joseph. Exodus pivots to the national aspect of Israel's story—crossing the sea, standing at Mount Sinai, and making the first leg of the journey to the Promised Land. Rabbi Hartman notes that the differences between the two books go beyond the distinction between the family story of Genesis and the national story of Exodus. He observes that the religious identities of the line of Abraham and Sarah are passed down or assumed—what sociologists would call identities of descent. Israelite identity in Exodus, on the other hand, is established by way of active covenantal commitments made by individuals. Jewish identity for Genesis Jews is an identity of being; Jewish identity for Exodus Jews is an identity of doing—by assent or consent.

Inspired by Hartman, I would propose an alternative prism through which to view the difference between Genesis Jews and Exodus Jews—the difference between the pull and push of tribal identity.

In Genesis, God's first call to Abraham is "Lekh l'kha": "Go forth to the land that I will show you. I will make of you a great nation, I will bless you, I will make your name great, and you shall be a blessing" (12:1–3). In broad brushstrokes, in the book of Genesis, Jewish identity is endowed by God and understood as a blessing bequeathed from one generation to the next; Jews are a distinct and distinctive people with a unique and prized relationship to God and to one another. Being Jewish is an identity that comes from within (or above), a freely given expression of one's being—the tug that binds an individual Jew to the wider Jewish community. Genesis is the positive pull of what it means to be a Jew.

As for Exodus Jews, one need go no further than the previously mentioned first verses of the book to see a very different expression of tribal identity: "And a new king arose over Egypt who did not know Joseph. And Pharaoh said to his people, 'Look, the Israelite people are much too numerous for us. Let us deal shrewdly with them . . . lest they join our enemies in fighting . . . So they set task-masters over them to oppress them" (Exodus 1:8–11). The transition is sharp and clear. In Exodus, Jews are designated as the "other." Jewish identity has switched from a self- or divinely assigned identity to one conferred by enemies. For Pharaoh and, by extension, the Egyptian people, the Israelites did not add anything to Egyptian society—just the opposite. Their presence evoked, as it will in the book of Esther, fears of a fifth column, fears that resulted in hatred, hatred that resulted in oppression.

As for the Israelites themselves, their sense of group identity was no longer anchored in the "positive pull"; now the "negative push" from those around them brought them together. Up until this point, to be an Israelite was considered a blessing, but now they were feeling the pinch and—soon enough—the "oppression" of otherhood.

What is a Genesis identity? A self-definition expressed

by way of voluntary acts of positive Jewish identification. What is an Exodus identity? A negative identity ascribed to Jews by others. This thesis is not airtight. There are Genesis elements in Exodus (Mount Sinai), and Exodus elements in Genesis. Nonetheless, the distinction is a helpful heuristic to understand the shifting dynamics of what it means to be a Jew—its inner pull and external push.

Prior to October 7th, most American Jews understood themselves to be Genesis Jews. The degree to which we observed Jewish life, affiliated with community, gave philanthropically, identified with Israel—these were all voluntary choices we made as individuals, as families, and as communities. We were no saints. For many, perhaps most, Jewish identity was more of a buffet than a prix-fixe menu, a series of episodic behavioral choices we opted into if we chose to do so, depending on the pull of our theological commitments, the communities into which we self-selected, or the degree to which we felt a sense of obligation through the pull of generational nostalgia. For non-Orthodox Jews, being Jewish was a lifestyle choice, an identity we asserted—or didn't. It was a product of living in a free society, in its blessings and challenges.

For diaspora Jewry, the attacks of October 7th created an abrupt transition from a life as Genesis Jews to Exodus Jews. The shock and violent brutality belied any notion that this was just the latest typical round of conflict between Israelis and Palestinians. As noted earlier, the pogrom-like nature of the day was intended as and understood to be an attack not just on Israel but on global Jewry. October 7th activated a world of "us versus them," triggering a long-dormant sense of global Jewish peoplehood. The divisions that had hitherto divided Jews—religious and nonreligious, left and right, for and against judicial reform—dissipated, at least for a moment. The Jewish people circled their wagons and coalesced.

Not joyfully; nor, for that matter, by our own volition. After October 7th, being a Jew became an identity defined by others, by those who ignore our pain, exclude us, hate us, threaten us, and in some cases kill us. An identity shaped by a fight on the battlefield in Israel and Gaza, against those who would deny our kin the sovereign right of self-defense and self-determination. An identity shaped by a fight on campuses, social media, and beyond. American Jewry has rallied to the calling of the hour, its sense of tribalism engaged, activated, and supercharged. On October 7th, American Jews became Exodus Jews, our Jewish identity shaped by our instinct for self-defense, in response to events tragic, traumatic, not of our choosing, and beyond our control. On October 7th and soon after, at least for many of us, whatever nuanced views we may have held regarding Israel became passé—to be a Jew meant to stand with Israel. American Jewry would have to be forgiven for this defensive posture.

The lack of clear distinction between the Judaism of American Jews and their engagement with Israel heightened the global challenge of October 7th—for us and our adversaries. More often than not, Israel's detractors—be it in the UN, the World Court, the streets of Europe, or any number of American college campuses—do not distinguish between the Jewish state and the Jews. The disruption of Jewish communal gatherings, the defacing of synagogues and campus Hillels, the verbal and physical intimidation aimed at American Jews qua Zionists set us back on our heels. Sometimes the antisemitic acts happened in far-off places: an angry mob at the airport in Russia's Dagestan region; graffiti scrawled on the walls of a Paris synagogue. Sometimes they occurred in the most familiar places—a doctor friend of mine jumped out of a New York City cab because of the antisemitic rantings of her driver. In all cases, these aggressions were aimed not just at Israel but at all Jews and Jewish interests. The fact that the Jewish state was being denied the right to self-defense and self-determination, a right that other sovereign states would surely claim without hesitation, revealed a double standard. This was another signal that the resistance to Israel's actions after October 7th was about more than Israel. It was about Jews themselves. As my friend and teacher Abe Foxman wrote, "Israel has become the Jew among the nations."

The offenses absorbed by American Jewry included both sins of commission and omission. American Jews well remembered progressives' fulsome embrace of the cause of Black lives in the wake of George Floyd's murder in 2020, and of Asian lives in the wake of the mass shootings of 2021. Those same communities failed to name the crimes of violence perpetrated against Jews on October 7th, even crimes of gruesome sexual violence. To us, it seemed that progressives believed that all lives, except Jewish ones, mattered. Why did it take the United Nations 150 days to validate the fact that sexual violence took place on October 7th? Why are the leaders of #BringBackOurGirls, who mobilized after the kidnapping of the schoolgirls in Chibok, Nigeria, not doing the same for the Israeli women and children taken as hostages? Do they not hear their own hypocrisy as they call for a ceasefire but not the release of hostages? Do they not realize that whatever their intent, chants of "From the River to the Sea—Palestine Must Be Free" will be heard as a call for the genocide of Israel's Jewish population?

As a congregational rabbi, since October 7th I have both borne witness to and experienced firsthand this transformation of identity, this loneliness caused by feeling "othered." It might be a slight—the slur directed at me one day as I walked, "yarmulke on," into the public library. It could be seeing the feeds of my fellow New York clergy—dear Christian friends whose calls for justice for the Palestinians somehow avoid mention of October 7th or the hostages. I want to be with people who "get me," "see me," and feel the same way I do. The two feelings are, to be sure, interdependent—two sides of the same coin. The "lean into community" serves as balm to our loneliness. Diaspora Jews are seeking to be in the company of people who confirm their spoken and unspoken commitments. Who *understand*. In a world that struggles to name evil for what it is, we are thirsting for a moral axis to the universe, where wrong can be named as such. We are seeking communities of positive Jewish expression. Shabbat dinners, synagogue attendance, philanthropy, adult learning, trips to Israel, public advocacy, rallies and marches—Jews are "doing Jewish" with other Jews in unprecedented numbers, over a sustained time. As one "old timer" in my community remarked to me in a crowded synagogue service, "Where did all these Jews come from?"

I often find myself in uncharted rabbinic territory. In the weeks following October 7th, I had scheduled an annual event, fall evening cocktails with parents of young children, for them to connect with clergy and community, and devote an evening to thinking intentionally about Jewish parenting. Attendance was exponentially larger than in previous years, my first indication that this evening would be different. I scrapped what I had prepared and opened the floor to hear what was on the minds of young parents. It was a world of heartbreak. Parents making choices about whether their children should or shouldn't wear yarmulkes or Star of David pendants. Parents with fears as to whether they can have open conversations about Jewish identity on buses and taxis and in other public places. One parent shared that she shushed her child as he ran out of the synagogue, singing Hebrew songs. "Rabbi," they asked me, "should they or shouldn't they wear outward signs of Jewish identity?" They were floored. I was floored. To live in New York City in 2024 and to be asking such questions— who could have thought that possible?

Another beloved tradition of mine is the sixth-grade book club, a chance for me to be in conversation with the children of our synagogue in the year prior to their bar and bat mitzvahs. One book we always read is *The Diary of Anne Frank,* which, for many children attending secular public or private schools, serves as their first introduction to the Holocaust. The students are always struck at how normal

Anne's secular childhood is at the book's beginning, only to be disrupted by the loss of non-Jewish friends, the wave of anti-Jewish restrictions, and eventually, her need to take refuge in the Secret Annex.

In the wake of October 7th, Anne's story took on new urgency for the children. One spoke of how she no longer speaks openly about her Jewishness in public spaces. Another related the hurtful and hate-filled comments she sees on social media—some from her friends and the parents of her friends. For better or for worse, much of a young person's reality today is constructed by way of social media and online presence. To be "blocked" by a friend or bombarded by anti-Israel posts is a heavy burden for a young person—for any person.

Perhaps the most dramatic change in my rabbinate since October 7th has been my interactions with the secular private schools that many children of my congregants attend. In the calculus of parenting choices made by American Jews, prep schools are considered a primary vehicle for social and educational advancement—a ticket to elite colleges and campus life, professional success, and integration into a progressive and pluralistic American dream. While much is gained by this type of education, it is an assimilatory move that is not without consequences. Jewish literacy, Jewish holidays, and points of Jewish identification and socialization take a backseat to secular commitments. Things as mundane as attending a homecoming dance on a Jewish holiday or choosing food from what is served in the school cafeteria—a million small and large decisions (and concessions) made along the way toward the larger goal of integration. To send a child to a secular private school does not signal rejection of Jewish identity—as a proud product of such an education, I can say with certainty that quite the opposite may be true; but it is, nonetheless, a significant choice in the balancing act of hyphenated identities.

But on October 7th, the cost of that choice came back to bite. The attacks made Jews feel like a vulnerable, persecuted minority. Surely we could rely on our schools to issue a sharp condemnation of Hamas's actions.

The responses made by those schools fell short. The countless school statements forwarded to me focused on anodyne prayers for peace and blanket condemnations of the "cycle of violence." At best, the parents in my congregation felt let down and lonely; at worst, they felt they were victims of antisemitism. For Jewish parents, the delayed, tepid, or equivocating responses of these schools signaled something deeper than letters poorly and perhaps too quickly drafted by a school's Diversity, Equity, and Inclusion administrator. This failing or rot—a betrayal, in fact, by the institutions to which parents had entrusted their children's education— had placed them in an unbearable situation.

I met with many school administrators; the majority were non-Jews, though some were Jewish. They were disoriented. Busy as they were, simply trying to make budgets and negotiate teacher contracts, they were neither well enough educated nor equipped to sort out the particulars of a conflict between Israel and Palestine. Many had never been to these places; a few of them couldn't locate them on a map. According to their worldview, Israel was a strong nation, and, following the progressive paradigm of the oppressors versus the oppressed, Israel was clearly among the former, not the latter. The fact that some of the schools' Jewish families made frequent trips to Israel seemed to indicate that Jews were privileged— international travel was, for example, a luxury beyond the reach of their scholarship students. In their minds, horrific as the attacks of October 7th were—a fact that no administrator denied—they were conducted in the context of a long-standing conflict, not justifiable but not without precedent. Most of all, these principals and heads of school were flummoxed, trying to get their heads around a new phenomenon in their schools—Jewish families who were suddenly assertive in their identity, publicly affirming in their Zionist commitments, and now perceived themselves to be persecuted. These school administrators would never have described these same parents and students in this way prior to October 7th.

I recall one such meeting with a head of school, who just wanted to get her bearings on the needs of the Jewish families she served. She had no real knowledge of or considered opinion on the Israeli-Palestinian conflict; nor, best as I could tell, did she have any bias one way or the other regarding Jews. She simply sensed that whatever response she made, it would fall short of the expectations of the Jewish parents. The time we scheduled together was not meant to be a pastoral meeting, but that is what it quickly became. With as much kindness and empathy as I could muster, I explained to her the post-October behavior of her Jewish families, making sure she knew she had a resource in me, should she ever need one.

Sympathetic as I was to that head of school, or any head of school, I understood why many of the parents among my congregants felt blindsided. Suddenly, they had been thrust out of the world of Genesis Jews and into what felt like the first verses of Exodus. "A new Pharaoh arose"—the oppression this time coming not by way of a taskmaster's whip but by the inability to identify their pain. I was well aware of the culture wars that had broken out on college campuses and have since spiraled out of control. What was happening on campus was also taking place on a smaller scale in high schools and middle schools.

The newfound assertiveness of Jewish identity is a response to the challenge and opportunity we currently face: to find a way to integrate the two strands of our identity, Exodus and Genesis. We need strength, we need stamina, and we need solidarity.

We are, without question, in an Exodus moment. We must find our front lines, the places where we, as individuals and as a community, can make a difference and fight the fight of our people—politically, philanthropically, and by other creative means. We must do all this . . . and we must never forget that we are also a people of Genesis—that this thing we are fighting for, Jews and Judaism, is a joy, a privilege, and a blessing to us and to all people. We must give of ourselves to defend Israel, and we must light Shabbat candles. We must go to ADL briefings on how to talk to our children about antisemitism, and we must take our children to synagogue so they come to love Shabbat and community. We must take our part in the curricular and cultural battles in our institutions of higher learning, and we must take Jewish learning to higher levels. We must celebrate our births, bnei mitzvah, and weddings, reminding one another, our children, and most of all ourselves of who we are. Jews must take agency—and joy—in their Judaism.

Put simply, to reduce my Jewish identity to fighting antisemitism is a victory I refuse to grant my foe. It was great to be a Jew on October 6, and it is still great to be a Jew today. Not just the push, and not just the pull, but the centripetal momentum of the two together—that is the generative force by which our community will be maintained.

Sometimes our tribal identity comes by way of a warm spark within. Sometimes the spark comes by way of an unsought and untoward force from without. I would, no question, choose the former over the latter any day, but the important thing is what we do when the spark comes. Is not our story today the story of Moses himself? Our greatest prophet was the most assimilated of Jews. He had grown up in Pharaoh's household, the adopted son of Pharaoh's own daughter. But when he sees the affliction of his Hebrew kinsman and the inaction of those around him, he steps up to save that kinsman and then, eventually, his whole people, leading us to a covenanted peoplehood of which we are still the beneficiaries today.

As a people of Genesis and Exodus, we must stand up and stand tall in defense of our people and never lose sight of the joy and the privilege that comes with being a Jew today. Our Jewishness comes from both the push and the pull. Neither one nor the other but the two together must inform who we are and what we will be in such a time as this.

EIGHT

FOR SUCH A TIME AS THIS

Esther, a Hero for Our Moment

The uptick in antisemitism following October 7th has been sharp, blindsiding us. But we do not have the luxury of being armchair sociologists. We have to respond. We have come together in the wake of the fear and hate unleashed on that day and begun to ask ourselves new questions. Is this a time to assert our Jewish identities or keep our heads down? Is it better to fight from within the halls of power or effectuate change from the outside? We have taken our Jewish identity for granted for so long. And now, for the first time in our lives, we have begun to ask, What kind of Jews do we want to be? Where do we turn for guidance in such a time as this?

This title of this book is taken from the biblical story of Esther—its setting, drama, and inner tensions speak to our time. Not so much the attacks of October 7th itself—there was no State of Israel in Esther's time—but the arc of its narrative and the inner and outer wrestling demanded of its central characters. It speaks to the assumptions we held, the rug pulled out from under us, and the path or possible paths forward. For such a time as this—Esther is the book by which to understand our moment.

Esther is one of five scrolls (megillot) found in the third section of the Hebrew Bible known as the Writings (Ketuvim). Not only is Esther one of the most beautifully crafted of all biblical literary creations, but also it bears certain features that make it rare, if not unique, in the biblical canon. First, and most obviously, its namesake and main character is a woman—no small thing in the boys' club of the Bible. Second, unlike every other biblical book, it does not contain the name of God. Third, and very important for our purposes, it tells the story of a Jewish community established outside Israel. Exiled from the land to Babylon in 586 BCE, the Jewish community had to reestablish itself under King Nebuchadnezzar, whose own empire would itself be conquered in 539 BCE by Persia's Cyrus the Great.

Interpreted and staged in plays commemorating the story and Purim, the holiday that celebrates it, at first blush Esther is an entertaining narrative about kings and queens and palace intrigue. Some find it a theological counterbalance to the rest of the Bible: the lack of God's name gives a hint that perhaps chance—not divine providence—governs the universe (the name Purim comes from the Hebrew for "lots," as in "to draw lots"). For others, it is a piece of proto-feminist literature documenting how two women—Esther and her royal predecessor, Vashti—negotiate the halls of patriarchy. It is also a political parable—a satire of sorts about the Persian regime, proximity to the throne, and the uses and abuses of power. Endlessly fascinating—

there are as many ways to interpret the story as there are readers.

At its most elemental, Esther tells the tale of a diaspora Jewish community navigating its status as a distinct minority in the majority culture of ancient Persia—a remarkable and remarkably relevant allegory by which to understand our present moment.

Having deposed Queen Vashti because of her refusal to appear at a royal banquet, King Ahasuerus issues an edict to bring forth every young maiden for consideration as the new royal consort. While this is remembered the world over as some sort of Miss Persia beauty pageant, a careful reading of the text suggests a more ambiguous and darker possibility. Was this palace call-up voluntary or coerced? For the maidens in question and their families, did it present an opportunity for social advancement or did it induce fear, like Pharaoh's decree against the firstborn in the book of Exodus? Not only are both readings plausible; they can exist side by side. Fear and opportunity—an occasion to "move up," in which much would be "given up."

On cue, Esther is introduced. Though her given name is Hadassah, her secular name is Esther, from the Hebrew word *astir,* meaning "I will hide." What Esther is hiding will become evident as the story progresses. Aside from Esther's physical beauty, we know only a few facts about her. First, she was orphaned; she is the ward of her foster father, Mordecai. Second, as a maiden in a man's world, her destiny is not her own to choose. Summoned by the king and directed to obey the summons by Mordecai, she

enters the royal pageant. Third, and perhaps most significant, she is a member of the Jewish community.

Mordecai is actually the first biblical figure to be called
a Jew—in Hebrew, Yehudi means "descended from the
tribe and land of Yehudah, or Judah." Prior to exile, no
distinction existed between national and religious identities. Only in the diaspora would Jews grapple with a more
complicated nature of what it meant to be a "Jew"; the
term was a new label and marker of identity. They were
citizens of their host country yet distinct as a people, with
their gaze ever directed to an ancestral land. One senses
that Esther's orphaned status was not just biological. Sepa-
rated from her land and family of origin, she was Jew-ish,
a Judean exile in King Ahasuerus's court.

Mordecai advises Esther to keep her Jewishness secret
when she enters the king's palace. Why she must do so
he never states, but Esther understands that her life will
be easier or safer (or both) if she hides her identity. Was it
easy or hard for Esther to keep her secret? Did she comply
under duress or in hope of advancement? The text never
really says. What the text does say is that in the months
to come, the transformation of her identity stretches beyond anything she could have imagined. The makeover
process, worthy of reality TV, was extraordinary both in
its intensity and duration: twelve months of oil and myrrh,
perfumes and women's cosmetics. Esther finds favor with
Hegai, one of the royal chamberlains, who furnishes Esther
with extra kindness, rations, and beauty aids. Whether
Esther's initial motivation was self-preservation or self-

promotion, she becomes acclimated to the comforts of her royal surroundings.

On the surface, Esther's yearlong makeover was intended to prepare her for an audience with the king. On a deeper level, the process enabled her to shed any vestiges of her national and religious origins. Known by her Persian name, orphaned by her parents, and exiled from her land, Esther, through marrying the king, had the opportunity to upwardly assimilate into her non-Jewish environs. Given the Bible's stance against intermarriage (especially of Israelite daughters to non-Israelite men), this feature of the story should not be glossed over or excused by way of rabbinic apologetics (for example, the claim that her marriage was coerced and thus not a violation of Jewish law). The fact that Ahasuerus was not just a king, but a non-Jewish king, seems to be the point—this is the ultimate and decisive act of assimilation. There is no going back. Her beauty and elegance win the day, she has found the king's favor, and the royal diadem is placed on her head. Esther survives the contest and now will thrive on the royal throne.

Esther has gained so much, but in doing so, she has also left much behind. One wonders how Esther felt when she looked at her mirror and saw a Persian queen staring back at her. She could "pass" as a non-Jew, something she may have imagined but never thought actually possible.

The first two chapters of Esther signal a comfortable and uneventful Jewish Persian existence, but in the third chapter the bottom falls out. Haman, a descendant of biblical Israel's historic enemy, Amalek, is promoted in the king's

court. Mordecai refuses to bow down to Haman, even at
the urging of the rest of the king's couriers. Mordecai's
behavior is perplexing. He has just advised Esther to hide
her identity—why does he take a different tack himself?
While later rabbinic interpreters suggest that in Mordecai's mind, such an act would have been akin to idolatry,
no such rationale is offered in the text itself. What is more,
the implications of Mordecai's refusal (like Vashti's earlier
refusal to appear before the king) extend beyond his own
personhood. Mordecai's actions as a self-identifying Jew
come to reflect on all the Jews and put his entire people
in danger. Could offering a small curtsy as Haman's procession passed really be so difficult? As uneasy as we felt at
Esther's immersion into Persian identity, we are puzzled
at Mordecai's stubborn refusal to give an inch to respect
the customs and norms of the Persian culture. Neither the
choice Esther nor Mordecai makes is perfect—both come
with cost and consequence.

Haman's wrath waxes hot. Lots are thrown, and a date
is set for the destruction of the Jews. Haman brings the
matter to the king:

> There is a certain people, scattered and dispersed
> among all the other peoples in all the provinces of
> your realm, whose laws are different from those of
> any other people and who do not obey the king's
> laws; and it is not in Your Majesty's interest to
> tolerate them. If it please Your Majesty, let an edict
> be drawn for their destruction.

(Esther 3:8–9)

∽

THE MOST SIGNIFICANT thing about Haman's message is not what he says, but what he doesn't say. He never mentions that the people in question are Jews. His objection is political in nature, not antisemitic. A fifth column exists within the kingdom, and Ahasuerus, operating out of willed ignorance or political expediency, gives the green light to destroy them. As news of the edict spreads through the kingdom, we read that the city of Shushan was "dumbfounded." Shushan's general population does not seem to bear Haman's Jew-hatred, but it would take a rare form of courage for an everyday Persian to raise an objection—Haman was probably counting on that. The virus of antisemitism needs only one point of entry to spread systemically. Haman understood that his hatred, combined with the king's enabling and a nation of bystanders, was all he needed to carry out his dastardly plans.

The decisive turning point arrives in the fourth chapter. Mordecai relays the ominous news of Haman's edict to Esther, imploring her to appeal to the king and plead on behalf of her people. Esther hedges, sending a message back to Mordecai stating that on penalty of death, she cannot enter the king's presence. Mordecai sends back a forceful reply:

Do not imagine that you, of all Jews, will escape with your life by being in the king's palace. If you keep silent in this moment, relief and deliverance will come to the Jews from another quarter, while

you and your father's house will perish. And who
knows, perhaps you have attained to a royal position
for such a time as this.

(Esther 4:13–14)

It is a sublime exchange, provoking tears every year I
hear it read—and thus the title of this book. The call for
agency has a through line back to Moses at the burning
bush, Abraham being called to the Promised Land, and the
primordial narratives of the Garden of Eden. This particular call to action comes not from God but from another
person, adding to its power and making it relatable to readers facing a decisive juncture in Jewish history—as we all
do in this post–October 7th world, in a time such as ours.

Mordecai seeks to persuade Esther in a number of ways.
Invoking the pull of peoplehood, Mordecai links Esther's
fate to that of her imperiled contemporaries and to her
ancestral roots. Like Moses, who, from the comfort of
Pharaoh's palace, identified with his kin—so too Esther.
Mordecai makes clear that her fate is tied to that of all
Jews. Her true identity will eventually come out, and even
her royal status will not offer protection. Both she and her
father's house will perish if the decree is enacted.

The judgment of history, Mordecai argues, rests upon
her. Should she remain silent, the Jews will be saved
through other means; but her inglorious inaction will
be remembered. Esther knows that both she and Mordecai know that, but for the chance events recounted in
prior chapters, she would not be sitting on a throne. Who
knows, Mordecai urges, if it was not "for such a time as

this" that Esther arrived at her royal station. Now is the time for moral courage.

And for the first time in this story, Esther takes action. Esther becomes the protagonist of her eponymous tale. She issues instructions to Mordecai to assemble all the Jews in order to participate in a fast on her behalf. Then, in a breach of protocol, and at great personal risk, she seeks an audience with the king. She knows she may perish, but she will no longer keep her identity *nistar*—hidden. Esther has come out from the shadows—a Jew, a woman, and a queen, she leans into all three aspects of her being.

Esther's "coming out" story appears to be framed by the earlier choices made by Mordecai and Vashti. Unlike Mordecai, whose public display of religious identity jeopardizes his people, Esther's public display of religious identity will save them. Unlike Vashti, who refused to appear before the king, Esther's heroism lies in the act of appearing, at great personal risk, before the king. Esther chooses to be an agent of change from within, not outside, the halls of power. Esther saved the Jews, but she did much more too. When it mattered most, she unapologetically claimed her roots, her station in life, and the right of her people to stand tall as citizens and Jews. She fearlessly asserts her identity on behalf of her people.

Esther's story stands as an enduring parable of Jewish identity. We recognize the inchoate nature of her early Jewishness, the "bargain" she makes to enter Persian society—adopting the accoutrements of secularization and shedding both the blessings and burdens of being part of a distinct people—and we see our story in hers. So too the whiplash moment of discovering the precarious nature of diaspora existence, with its combination of haters, enablers, and bystanders—that also strikes close to home. We feel for Esther as she squirms in her indecision: "Is this really my fight? I could lose so much, even my life. Besides, who am I to turn the tide of history?" Esther's story and Esther's struggle are very much our own. And we can turn to her for guidance. Esther risks it all: power, popularity, prestige, and social acceptance; she risks her own life for the life of her people. Esther didn't choose her moment; it chose her. And when the moment came, she put herself on the line, threw her lot in with her people, and rallied them to action. A heroine for her time. A heroine for our time.

Ours is an Esther moment. We too have made bargains with modernity; we too have adapted to our host culture, only to discover that we are not quite as much at home as we thought we were. Who knows if it was not for such a moment as this that we arrived at our station in life? We can't know for sure, but we dare not risk being on the wrong side of history. Some things are better not left to chance. Today and every day, may we be ready to stand proud as Jews, to pass the test as Esther did, and to courageously respond whenever the safety and security of our people hang in the balance.

NINE

KIY'MU V'KIBLU

Affirming and Accepting
Our Jewish Identity

At first blush, the book of Esther does not appear to be the obvious place to begin a conversation on the performance of *mitzvot*—the observances, or "commandments," of Jewish practice. While the arc of the narrative tracks along the question of Jewish identity, nothing indicates that Esther, Mordecai, or any other of the Jewish inhabitants of the city of Shushan, in ancient Persia, led religiously observant lives. Their Jewish identities were civic or cultural in nature, defined by the degree to which they were accepted (or not) by the non-Jewish society in which they lived. Whether they observed the commandments of Shabbat or kashrut (dietary laws) or otherwise is never stated. Today we might call them "culturally identified" Jews, perhaps members of their local JCCs and occasional donors to their Jewish Federations—what contemporary sociologists of religion would call "Jews of no religion."

All of which is why it is remarkable that in the later rabbinic imagination, the entire edifice of mitzvot hinges on the book of Esther—one verse specifically. The central drama has concluded; Haman is dead and Mordecai has gone forth, in royal apparel, from the presence of the king. Having averted disaster and successfully defended themselves against their enemy, the Jews of Shushan enjoyed "orah v'simchah, sasson v'yikar," "light and gladness, joy and honor" (Esther 8:16). Mordecai, now elevated in stature, issues dispatches throughout the kingdom for the observance of the Purim festival—a time of feasting, merrymaking, and gift giving to one another and to the poor:

> The Jews affirmed and accepted (kiy'mu v'kiblu ha-yehudim) upon themselves and their descendants, and all who might join them, to observe these two days [of Purim] in the manner prescribed and at the proper time each year.
>
> *(Esther 9:27)*

The text is rather straightforward—seemingly, it's just a footnote affirming that the Jews of that generation accepted the laws of Purim. But in the hands of the rabbinic sages, this verse takes on extraordinary and enduring legal significance. We must make a short detour into Jewish law to see how this happened.

When the children of Israel stood at the base of Mount Sinai to receive the Ten Commandments and the rest of the law from Moses, their acceptance, according to the rabbinic sages, occurred under duress. The rabbis suggest that the Israelites did not stand at the base of the mountain, but rather beneath it—literally—with God holding it up above their heads. "This teaches, continues the rab-

binic midrash [commentary] that the Holy One, Blessed
be He, covered them with the mountain . . . and said to
them 'If you accept the Torah—well and good. And if not,
there will be your burial'" (Talmud Shabbat 88a). In such
a telling, God, like the cinematic Godfather, Don Corle-
one, made them an offer they couldn't refuse. Colorful as
this rendition may be, it raises a legal problem—how can a
covenant be binding if made under duress? How can future
generations be bound by mitzvot (commandments) if they
were initially accepted under coercion?

In order to solve this conundrum, the rabbis turned to
our verse in the book of Esther: "The Jews affirmed and
accepted (kiy'mu v'kiblu ha-yehudim)"; in other words, they
affirmed (in the time of Ahasuerus) what they had already
accepted (under duress—in the time of Moses). Our verse
thus refers not to any specific set of Purim laws, but rather
to the entire corpus of Jewish law, which is binding not
just for Esther's generation, but for all generations. In other
words, for the centuries following Mount Sinai itself, Jews
may have been coerced to accept the law, but from the time
of Esther onward, Israel accepted the covenant freely, of its
own volition. It thus became binding for all generations to
come, to this very day.

As such, the book of Esther carries extraordinary significance for Jewish identity. It contains a meditation on
the vulnerability of Jews and the rise of antisemitism, yet
it also becomes the base text on joyful and positive assertions about our Judaism and being a Jewish community.
The book tells the gripping and inspiring story of the way
Esther foiled Haman's plans, but it is also the urtext for

living a proud Jewish life. Interestingly, this paradigm did not arise at Mount Sinai, nor, for that matter, in the land of Israel. It came about in a diaspora Jewish community living under the threat of destruction.

Our moment is altogether analogous to the time of Esther. Faced as we are with the prospect of a world inhospitable to Jewish identity, where the line between anti-Zionist and antisemitic sentiment is blurred, where the Jewish people themselves may be divided concerning the terms and substance of diaspora Jewry's relationship with Israel, the case for a return to the basics of Jewish life and living—mitzvot—is more compelling than ever.

The headwinds to securing a positive and affirming expression of Jewish life, to be sure, long preceded October 7th. The number of "Jews of no religion" has been experiencing a precipitous uptick, more so that any particular Jewish denomination (Orthodox, Conservative, Reform, and so on). According to a 2020 Pew study, 40 percent of American Jews under the age of thirty eschew faith commitments and discernible patterns of observance; they consider themselves "ethnically" or "culturally" Jewish. Like the Jews of Esther's time, they may publicly affirm their identity as Jews, yet are removed from our religion, the wellspring of our identity.

Uncomfortable as it is to discuss, the impoverished condition of the religion of many diaspora Jews sits in plain view. We are more at home with debating the Iran deal and the grades of uranium that can be weaponized than we are with opening a prayerbook. We make every effort to understand the opportunity and challenge of critical race theory, but we are flat-footed when asked what it means to stand in a covenantal relationship with God. We are willing to drive for hours to stand on the sidelines at our children's club sports, but we find ourselves unable (or unwilling) to sit next to them in synagogue on a Friday night or a Shabbat morning. We will try any fad diet other than the one prescribed by our Torah. We would rather label another a "self-hating Jew" or a "settler-colonialist" than acknowledge that our children or grandchildren have no ostensible connection to Judaism, never mind the State of Israel.

As important as nonreligious expressions of Judaism may be, they are entirely insufficient to transmit the riches of Judaism from one generation to the next. In many cases, the secular commitments of Jews serve as compensatory guilt offerings, hiding paper-thin religious identities. In all cases, they presuppose a commitment to Judaism that, for much of diaspora Jewry, is not as vital as we would care to admit. My concern is that a Judaism without the foundation of religion will prove to be our undoing, a giant sinkhole into which the hard-earned superstructure supporting diaspora Jewry will collapse.

Only by way of mitzvot, the positive acts of Jewish identification, the language and behaviors of the Jewish religion, can Judaism survive. Mitzvot are the mystic chords, the commitments and commandments by which one Jew connects to another—and, belief permitting, to God.

For the spiritually minded, mitzvot are the gestures that we make, the rituals we do, to express our vertical relationship to the divine. The relationships in my life that mean the most to me—with my wife, my parents, my children—defy words. So I express my commitment in deeds, in actions—daily, weekly, and seasonally—that reflect the covenantal bonds that we share. It is simply beyond my ability to give voice to all the joy of being alive and, when faced with the unspeakable sorrow that I experience when I recognize the limits of my humanity, I have no words—so I turn to mitzvot.

Mitzvot make the mundane sacred, the agonizing tolerable, and the presence of God palpable when I need it most and feel it least. Louis Finkelstein, the late chancellor of the Jewish Theological Seminary, reflected: "When I pray, I speak to God; when I study Torah, God speaks to me." When I light Shabbat candles, when I put on my tefillin (phylacteries) every weekday in my morning prayers, when I refrain from eating off one side of the menu in favor of the other in order to follow the dietary laws of keeping kosher, I am—to use the language of Rabbi Abraham Joshua Heschel—taking a leap of action.

Even for those to whom appeals to the divine are a leap too far, a life of mitzvot remains the most assured means to inspire individual and collective Jewish identity and continuity—a connection to the Jewish people by way of religious expression. We light the same Shabbat candles, we sing the same (or similar) prayers, we read the same books, and we observe the same festivals as the Jews who came before us, those who are alive today, and those who will come after us.

The great twentieth-century thinker Rabbi Mordecai Kaplan spoke of mitzvot as folkways—the shared customs of Jewish civilization. Every community has its folkways, the behaviors and regimens—daily, seasonal, annual—that bind individuals together. Folkways that mark the passage of time and personal transformations connect us to a past long preceding us and a future well beyond the horizon of our brief years. Mitzvot are the sacred shibboleths by which Jews build conscious community, the vessels of transmission by which Jewish identity is passed on—the Proustian madeleines, the triggers to memory that have kept our people together across continents and generations.

There are all sorts of reasons to observe mitzvot, not the least of which is, speaking personally, that I quite enjoy them. Always, but especially since becoming an empty nester, I literally count the days between one Shabbat to the next, when our Sabbath table will be filled with old and new friends. Mitzvot are positive, joyful, and volitional acts of Jewish self-identification.

The positive and open expression of your Jewish self: that is the argument for a mitzvah. As American Jews, we are accustomed to being approached by a member of the Chabad outreach organization. "Excuse me, are you Jewish?" we are asked, as we pass by on the street. And then, the follow-up, if you are a man: "Would you like to put on tefillin?" Or, if you are a woman: "Would you like to learn how to light Shabbos candles?" It is worth considering the choreography of the "ask." It is actually an offer, an invitation, perhaps even a challenge. Will you, by way of performing this distinctly Jewish act, this mitzvah, please self-identify as a Jew? Performing a mitzvah is a proud transformation of the universal self into a Jewish self, making manifest one's particular identity through decisions about what to eat, how to structure one's time, and how to present oneself to the world.

Why observe mitzvot? Because doing so is the means by which one expresses pride in one's Jewishness, where one has come from and the hope that those who come after will feel and do the same. There is no greater act of Jewish self-assertion, empowerment, and hope than the performance of a mitzvah. To do a mitzvah is to take agency for one's spiritual life.

The lives of contemporary Jews are full of mitzvot, and not just Jewish ones. We need to take the same agency in our spiritual lives that we do in the rest of our lives. Nor, for that matter, are mitzvot the domain of Orthodox Jews. The great twentieth-century Jewish thinker Franz Rosenzweig, when asked whether he put on tefillin, replied, "Not yet." The task at hand is how to move spiritual living along a path from "not my thing," to "not yet," to "why not, let's see what happens." "Taste and see," teaches the psalmist (Psalm 34:9). We must be open to the possibility of performing one holy deed and seeing what happens next.

Now is the time to remind ourselves and the world of the joyful and willed choice of being, as described in chapter 7, a "Genesis Jew." The famed Green Bay Packers coach Vince Lombardi taught that "the best defense is a great offense." Now is an opportune time to operationalize a cross-communal effort to recover and reclaim the language and practice of mitzvot. In an era of podcasts, Pelotons, and "Couch to 5K" training programs, the Jewish community surely can figure out a way to bolster the individual and communal performance of Judaism as a religion—a *kiy'mu v'kiblu*, affirmation and acceptance—for such a time as this.

Preliminarily, such an effort could be framed by way of four rubrics described here:

HEAD. For the vast majority of American Jews, the language of mitzvot is a closed book. What are the rhythms of the Jewish year? How has Jewish practice developed over the ages? What are the great books of our tradition? This is not creation ex nihilo—generations of Jewish educators have devoted careers to creating accessible curricula. The task of our time is to update and recast the efforts of our predecessors in a manner consistent with the best practices and platforms by which educational content is accessed today.

HEART. Our lives have a limited and indeterminate length. How can they best be filled with meaning and purpose? How am I connected to those who came before me, and what is the legacy I leave to those who will follow? How shall I balance the particularism of my Jewish identity with my universal commitments to a shared humanity? What is it that the Lord requires of me? Rabbis and Jewish educators (and the institutions that train them) must inspire contemporary Jewry to adopt mitzvot as the historic and ever-evolving toolbox for exploring the existential questions within all our hearts.

HOW-TO. The greatest impediment to Jewish practice is neither theological nor ideological, but practical. How do

I recite kiddush—the Sabbath blessing over wine? When exactly do I bow in a synagogue service? Where can I learn Hebrew? How do I host a discussion on the Torah reading at my Shabbat table—or host a Shabbat dinner at all? The gap between American Jewry's vaunted secular educational achievements and its anemic Jewish literacy is daunting but not insurmountable. Instructional TikToks and You-Tube videos abound for everything from cooking to yoga, so why not populate the internet with how-to content on the greatest spiritual practice of all—Judaism? Such curricula must be judgment-free, affirming the varied paths by which individuals today seek entry into the tradition.

COMMUNITY. Critical as the aforementioned three rubrics are to motivating Jewish observance, only communal reinforcement will make it all stick. One-on-one mentorship, interconnected *havurot* (small communities), online engagement, and intensive, retreat-based education can together provide the ecosystem to nurture and sustain the desired outcomes in Jewish practice. Intentional communities (modeled after the success of programs such as One Table and Honeymoon Israel) should be conceived and implemented in partnership with the existing structures of American communal life. Synagogues, Hillels, and other legacy institutions are already poised to serve the needs of contemporary Jewry, and they stand to be the primary beneficiaries of reinvigorated religious practice.

Head, heart, how-to, and community: this is preliminary vocabulary for a program to restore the religion of Judaism to the Jewish people, an effort that could be shared by Israel and the diaspora, across denominations and political divides. Indeed, in an era as polarized as our own, the shared rallying cry of world Jewry to return to a religion of mitzvot is a dividend worthwhile in itself.

"A community cannot survive on what it remembers," wrote the late Conservative rabbi and scholar Arthur Hertzberg. "It will persist only because of what it affirms and believes." It is our religion that has kept us as Jews, defined us as a people, and that is the key to Jewish continuity. It will require an undertaking of no small significance to reverse current trends and empower American Jews to reclaim their religious heritage, in all its manifold varieties. In the wake of October 7th, I am hard-pressed to think of a project more urgent, necessary, or exciting.

We are capable and ready to take the initial steps to launch these programs (as we are doing in my synagogue). As in the story of Esther, it all comes down to human agency. Will we model the values and behaviors that will inspire and motivate others to join in this work?

I recall walking to synagogue with my daughter, then five years old (and now a college graduate). As we walked hand in hand, I turned to her and said, "You know what, Lucy, here we are walking hand in hand to shul together. When I was a little boy, I walked to shul holding my daddy's, your grandpa's, hand. And you know what is even more interesting? When grandpa was a little boy, he walked to shul holding his daddy's hand." On and on I went—confident that she had lost interest in what I found to be so interesting—until she tugged at my hand, looked up at me, and asked, "Daddy, did Moses walk to shul with his children?" I answered her in the only way I knew how: "Yes, Lucy. Moses walked to shul with his children."

For lack of a magic elixir to ensure the continuity of the Jewish faith and people, the best we can do is take agency, play our particular and special role. To reach out our hand to our children, with the hope that they extend theirs in return. To practice our faith, spend more time showing and less time telling. Step by step, hand in hand, mitzvah to mitzvah, generation to generation.

EMPATHY OR REVENGE

Choosing a Path of Peace

L ike the royal diadem that sat atop her crown, the story of Esther casts its light in kaleidoscopic directions, offering endless take-home messages.

A tale about diaspora Jewry, a fight against assimilation as well as antisemitism, a proto-feminist leadership story, and, as noted in the prior chapter, an affirmation of the power of a positive expression of Jewish life and living. The book of Esther is a magnificent literary creation that continues to inspire, with its every Purim reading. For such a time as this—and at every time—Esther is filled with rich interpretive possibilities.

Any discussion of Esther, however, would be incomplete without at least noting its dark underside, an underside which, by way of another memory of mine in Israel, speaks with alarming urgency today, in the wake of the October 7th attacks.

I can recall with great clarity exactly where I was on Purim, February 25, 1994. I was living in Israel that year, on a gap-year program after college. It was a Friday. I had a free weekend in honor of the Purim holiday, and I was standing at a bus stop on my way to see a cute girl I had met a few months earlier. (Her name was Debbie and she would one day become my wife.) This was before cell phones, so I had to use the bus-stop pay phone to call my Israeli host family and wish them *shabbat shalom*. My host mother, Shari, broke the horrific news to me. A Jewish extremist named Baruch Goldstein had entered Hebron's Cave of the Patriarchs and killed 29 Muslim worshippers; he also wounded more than 125.

What happened next is a bit of a blur. I remember Shari telling me, in no uncertain terms, that I needed to be careful and steer clear of public spaces because Goldstein's murderous rampage would undoubtedly unleash a violent Arab response. Israel's prime minister, Yitzhak Rabin, called Yasser Arafat, the Palestinian leader, describing the attack as a "loathsome, criminal act of murder"; Rabin also publicly denounced Goldstein on the floor of the Knesset as a "shame on Zionism and an embarrassment to Judaism." Nevertheless, the anger on the streets overflowed. In the days that followed, Palestinian protests and riots broke out, during which five Israelis and twenty-five Palestinians were killed. The violence, the fear, the calls back and forth to my parents, who wanted to make sure I was okay—I remember it all, always, but especially every year when Purim is celebrated.

Vivid as my memories are, what I didn't understand then was the *reason* (though that word hardly fits) why Goldstein chose the holiday of Purim as the moment for his heinous act. When we think of Purim, festivity and fun come to mind—costumes, hamantaschen, groggers, and

Purim spiels. We let down our hair, we poke fun at each other. There is a commandment to drink, and participants are asked to fulfill the mitzvah of giving gifts to each other and to the poor. Most of all, Purim is the day when we read the story of Esther. Mordecai refuses to bow down to Haman, and Haman lays dastardly plans to kill all the Jews of Shushan. These plans are foiled by the courageous and beautiful Esther, who, at the critical moment, saves the day by revealing her Jewish identity to King Ahasuerus. A day marked for the destruction of Jews is transformed into one of salvation—the Jews enjoy "light and gladness, happiness and honor" (Esther 8:16). As noted in the prior chapter, the Jews of Shushan affirm their Jewish identity, for themselves and for the generations to come.

But that is not the whole story. Toward its conclusion, things go sideways and dark. Some may recall that Haman and his ten sons are impaled on the stake. But that's not all. What happens next, in chapter 9, is rarely taught in Hebrew school classrooms. The text states the Jews of Persia rose up to attack all those who had sought to do them harm. In the city of Shushan, five hundred were killed (in addition to Haman and his sons), and three hundred more the following day. And, in a staggering bloodbath, Jews killed seventy-five thousand people in the rest of Persia. Understandably, we rarely spotlight Esther's ending. For obvious reasons, we don't teach it to kids, but it is part of the story—no more and no less than Vashti's character, Esther's beauty, and Haman's wickedness.

And the sentiment of this chapter is also expressed elsewhere. On the Shabbat before Purim, called Shabbat

Zakhor, the Sabbath of Remembrance, verses are included that contain the commandment to wipe out Amalek, blotting out the memory of Haman's entire line—the enemies, past, present, and future, who would seek the downfall of the Jews. It is a lot to swallow—a fanciful tale of kings and queens turned into a nightmare of vengeance.

I have always excused the ninth chapter of Esther as a literary embellishment not to be taken literally, some sort of gruesome fantasy devised by the author in response to the near destruction of the Jews at the hands of Haman. A fantasy whereby a disempowered author imagines gaining power over the oppressors. It is akin to the moment (discussed in chapter 4) during the Passover seder when we open the door for Elijah to read *Sh'foch Hamat'kha* "pour out your wrath" upon the nations; a downtrodden people thumbing their nose at their oppressors. For those with a cinematic bent, it's a bit like Quentin Tarantino's 2009 *Inglourious Basterds,* a brutal movie about an alternative, purgative reality in which Hitler and his henchmen are themselves violently killed. Generations of oppressed Jews have turned to the story of Esther and to the holiday of Purim as a vehicle to express violent fantasies of what they would do to those Jew-hating non-Jews if they only had the power.

But for a right-wing extremist zealot like Baruch Goldstein, the fantasy of Esther in chapter 9 was no fantasy; it was a biblical proof text, giving him license, or even commanding him, to perform an act of vengeance. In Goldstein's twisted and murderous mind, the Jewish collective memory of oppression, together with the continued presence of antisemitism, prompted him to violent action. Goldstein's spiritual godfather was a man named Meir Kahane, an idealogue of such noxious and racist hatreds that he and his dogmatic beliefs were outlawed by Israel's Knesset in the 1980s. And Baruch Goldstein had the power to take lives: specifically, a Gillon assault rifle and 140 rounds of ammunition. In the words of the philosopher Yehuda Elkana, Goldstein felt obligated to go beyond the assertion "never again"; he chose "never again to us," even if that meant shedding further blood. Goldstein did not leverage the Jewish historical memory of persecution to develop a sense of empathy—just the opposite. Why did Goldstein commit mass murder against non-Jews on Purim? Because his theology was founded not on the empathy of the book of Exodus but on the hatreds in the book of Esther—a messianic vision stemming from the fear of Jewish powerlessness, to which, gun in hand, he gave murderous expression.

Goldstein was beaten to death that day by survivors of his attack, but his ideology did not die. Although the Israeli military authorities denied him burial in a Jewish cemetery, his gravesite has become a pilgrimage site for Jewish extremists. The epitaph on his tombstone refers to him as a martyr who died with clean hands and a pure heart.

Far more worrisome to me than the location of his remains is the fact that his spirit lives on. If anything, the traumas against the Jews, up through and including October 7th, tend to give rise to more hatred.

We need not look far to see the Hamans of our time, those who seek the destruction of the Jews. In a post–

October 7th world, the masks have come off, and the enemies of the Jewish people stand exposed—in Israel, in
the Middle East, in Europe, in America, from the political
right to the left. The threats are real. We are not wrong
to feel vulnerable. The world's most ancient hatred is alive
and well today—online, on the streets, and on the world
stage. The Jew being made "other," depicted as menacing,
powerful, and threatening, is then rendered an object of
hatred and violence.

We must stand vigilant; we must fight to secure the
well-being of our people in the diaspora and in Israel; and
the perpetrators of violence against our people must be
brought to justice. In this moment, and always.

And, at the same time, we must never, ever let the historical memory and lived reality of antisemitism provide
cover for violent excesses, of an unhinged messianic abuse of
Jewish power. Well prior to October 7th, on February 26,
2023, vigilante settlers rampaged through the Palestinian
town of Huwara in the West Bank, committing an out-
rage in breach of every human and Jewish value. It was
outrageous that it happened; that the perpetrators were
not brought to justice; and that Bezalel Smotrich, a high-
ranking minister in Israel's government, subsequently
called for the entire town of Huwara to be "wiped out."

Israel must never fall prey to the perils of unchecked
vengeance. The fabric of Israeli society is already stretched
to its limit, and I am frightened as to what might happen if
the tinderbox of the Jewish state is ignited by the fraught
theology of the final chapters of Esther. It is not merely
that the specter of Baruch Goldstein and the hateful ide-

ology he espoused continue to loom large. Until not long ago, Itamar Ben-Gvir, Israel's minister of national security, kept a framed picture of Baruch Goldstein on his wall. Ben-Gvir is not a fringe figure—just the opposite. His ministry oversees the police. He too is an admirer of the self-same Kahanist ideology that gave rise to Baruch Goldstein. It is enough to keep me up at night. It should be keeping all of us up at night.

Jews, to be sure, are not the only people for whom the memory of persecution and victimization has been leveraged toward acts of violent aggression. The example of the Serbs is but one that comes to mind. But the Jews, perhaps more than any other people, would be well-advised to consider how the memory of victimization, when combined with the apparatus of state power, can lead to violent injustices perpetrated against others.

As Jews, we do not turn the other cheek, but we must ever consider the possibility that tomorrow can be better than today. To live by the maxim that "those to whom evil is done do evil in return" is to resign ourselves to an unbreakable cycle of violence. As the Reverend Martin Luther King Jr. preached: "Returning hate for hate multiplies hate, adding deeper darkness to a night already devoid of stars. Darkness cannot drive out darkness; only light can do that. Hate cannot drive out hate; only love can do that."

Will our vision for the Jewish people stem from fear, hatred, and demonization of the other, or will we commit ourselves to a vision and a path of dialogue, trust, and bridge building? Will we turn inward, crouching tightly into a defensive posture, or will we stretch ourselves beyond our comfort zone, and seek to build a better future? Will our experience of Jewish vulnerability, and the horrors of October 7th, be leveraged as a moral cudgel to excuse indiscriminate Jewish violence, or will it be a prompt for empathy and concern for all human suffering?

Esther's messages are manifold. Its most important may be its darkest: a cautionary tale of the path we must not take. Perhaps it is precisely in such a time as this, filled as we are with pain, that we must remember that what we choose *not* to do is more important than what we choose to do. We can be strong but not vengeful, self-assured but never bloodthirsty, and ever seeking *shalom*—peace.

ELEVEN

SINAT ḤINAM

Why Our Greatest Risk Is the Enemy Within

On account of baseless hatred, the Talmud teaches (Gittin 55b), Jerusalem was destroyed, and the Jewish people exiled from their land. The most famous rabbinic tale regarding the dangers of the hatreds from "within" is found in the Talmud in reference to the time leading up to the destruction of Jerusalem's Second Temple at the hands of the Romans in 70 CE.

A rich man lived in Jerusalem who had a dear friend named Kamtza and a sworn enemy named Bar Kamtza. The rich man decided to host a banquet and instructed his servant to deliver an invitation to all his friends, including Kamtza. The servant, however, mistakenly delivered the invitation to his master's enemy—Bar Kamtza. On the night of the party, the rich man saw his enemy enter his home, and he confronted him, demanding that Bar Kamtza leave the banquet immediately.

"Please," said Bar Kamtza, "I am already here. Do not embarrass me. Allow me to stay, and I will pay for anything I eat and drink."

"Absolutely not," replied the host. "Get out of my house!"

"I beg of you," said Bar Kamtza, "let's not make a scene. Allow me to stay, and I will pay for half of the party." Once again the host refused.

One last time Bar Kamtza pleaded, this time offering to pay for the entire gathering, if only he could be saved from public disgrace. The stone-hearted host refused and had Bar Kamtza forcibly removed.

Shamed before those in attendance, Bar Kamtza left, fuming at being so ill-treated. His humiliation turned to anger, which in turn was transformed into a desire for vengeance. The Talmudic story explains that Bar Kamtza then reported to the Roman emperor that a rebellion was brewing among the Jews. This (to make a long story short) set in motion the siege of Jerusalem, the decimation of the Jewish leadership, the destruction of the Temple, and, eventually, the exile of the Jewish people from our land.

There is so much about the story worth unpacking. Why was it that the host could not see past his grudge? How did things spiral so badly out of control? What about all the guests in attendance who watched the debacle unfold— why didn't anyone intervene? It is a tale about the dangers of excessive ego, the obligation to be an upstander rather than a bystander, and a reminder of the role each person plays in maintaining the social fabric of a healthy and vital community.

Most pointedly, the story assigns blame for the down-fall of ancient Israel on Israel, not on an external enemy, Roman or otherwise. This cautionary tale reveals the dangers of infighting among our people; it brings about a self-inflicted trauma and the most horrific outcome our rabbis could imagine—the end of the sovereign Jewish state.

The rabbis were well attuned to the consequences of a society incapable of housing dissent—that it was important to disagree without allowing those disagreements to be the undoing of our people. Throughout Jewish history, our people have never lacked for external enemies. From the oppression of Pharaoh, to the pogroms of our exile, to the darkest hours of Nazi persecution, to the wars Israel fights today—our enemies have been real, existential, and persistent. Nevertheless, it was *sinat ḥinam*—baseless hatred—which the rabbis most feared would lead to our undoing.

Sinat ḥinam comes when we harden our hearts to one another, when we demonize our disagreements, when those disagreements deepen and become entrenched, when the humanity of the person with whom we disagree is eclipsed. Then terrible events inevitably ensue. *Sinat ḥinam* is the enemy from within, which, through the eyes of Jewish history, is our greatest threat.

In my own life, it is not the destruction of the Temple but rather the assassination of Israel's prime minister, Yitzhak Rabin, in 1995 that will forever represent the dangers of baseless hatred. As I noted in chapter 3, I was studying in Israel that year, as part of my rabbinic training. Word of the tragedy quickly spread throughout Israel. Eitan Haber, the prime minister's bureau chief, stood outside the gates of Tel Aviv's Ichilov Hospital and declared that Rabin had died on the operating table: "With horror, great sorrow, and deep grief, the government of Israel announces the

death of Prime Minister and Defense Minister Yitzhak
Rabin, murdered by an assassin, tonight in Tel Aviv. The
government shall convene in one hour for a mourning ses-
sion in Tel Aviv. May his memory be a blessing."

On the night of his assassination, November 4, 1995,
hundreds of thousands had gathered in Tel Aviv's Kikar
Malkhei Yisrael for a massive pro-peace rally. "I was a soldier for twenty-seven years," said Rabin in a booming voice.
"I believe there is a chance for peace. A great chance which
must be seized. Violence is undermining the foundations of
Israeli democracy . . . it must be rejected and condemned,
and it must be contained. It is not the way of the State of
Israel. Democracy is our way. There may be differences,
but they will be resolved in democratic elections . . ."

Rabin's final remarks became immediately and horrif-
ically prophetic: he was shot minutes later by an ultra-
nationalist Jewish terrorist.

In the months to come, investigative panels reported
that the assassination resulted from a complete collapse
of security. But what we all understood then, and all the
more so now, was that Rabin's murder reflected the break-
down of something far more substantive than security
protocol. There had been inflammatory rhetoric in the
months leading up to the assassination. Bumper stickers
read, "Rabin is a traitor." Leaflets depicted Rabin dressed
as a Nazi SS officer. There were deliberations in the right-
wing religious community as to whether Rabin's actions
were such a threat to Jewish life that the taking of his life
could find justification within Jewish law. Rabin's murder
signaled Israel's inability to house internal dissent. It was

a moment when one Jew became so unshakably convinced of the rightness of his own convictions that he denied the right of another Jew to hold others, and in so doing, denied him of his very life. A bullet may have killed Rabin—but it was the *sinat ḥinam* in the heart of the assassin that pulled the trigger.

Rabin's murder was a turning point in Israel's history—arguably, one from which it has never recovered, every moment since a "counterfactual" had this warrior-turned-peace-advocate been given the chance to see his vision find fruition. Unlike the time of the Romans, thank goodness, Israel was able to survive. And yet the lesson it carries—the price the Jewish people pay for infighting—has not yet been learned.

If I had to identify the pathology of our present moment, it would be our combative rhetoric and pervasive incivility. Discourse has gotten worse, not better, since 1995. In America, in the Middle East, within Israel, often in our own families, the particulars may differ, but the defect is one and the same. We have allowed self-interest to eclipse our common humanity; the orthodoxies of our agendas prevent us from striving toward the greater good.

In his classic work *Civilization and Its Discontents*, Sigmund Freud explained what caused cultures, nations, or religions to turn against each other, using a felicitous expression: "the narcissism of minor differences." Due to their vanity and self-absorption, people inflate minor disagreements at the expense of forming potentially greater relationships. We do this all the time, in counterproductive and self-destructive ways, yet insist that we are acting in defense of principle. But the only thing we are really defending is our ego.

Long before Freud, the rabbis of old well understood that as important as "what" we debate is "how" we debate. A passage in Pirkei Avot (The Ethics of the Fathers) makes a distinction between two kinds of debate—those "for the sake of heaven" and those that are not. What is an argument for the sake of Heaven? The argument between Hillel and Shammai. What is an argument not for the sake of Heaven? The argument of Korach and his company (Pirkei Avot 5:17).

A little background: The latter argument, that of Korach and his company, refers to an internal rebellion that took place during ancient Israel's wilderness wandering. Whatever the merits of the ideas held by the faction of Korach against the leadership of Moses were, the rabbis understood their inflammatory rhetoric to be less about the quest for truth and more about their own egos and pursuit of power—the vanity and self-absorption that Freud described centuries later.

An argument "for the sake of Heaven," on the other hand, is that of Hillel and Shammai. In the classic Talmudic debates between these two schools—those of Hillel and Shammai—the rabbis recall that they disagreed on just about everything: matters of law, practice, and theology. And yet, we are told that children from the two schools married one another. In "rabbinic speak," they understood themselves, no matter their differences, as one community (Yevamot 14a). Elsewhere in the Talmud, the rabbis specifically highlight the manner in which Hillel debated; he was remembered not just for what he said, but how he said it. He *always* dignified the merits of the opposing side by stating its view before offering his own opinion.

Hillel sought truth. He did not presume to hold it. He argued for the sake of knowing the Will of Heaven, even if it were to be forever elusive. As much as the rabbis prized a culture of debate, they understood themselves not as embodiments of truth but as instruments that approximated, or approached, the divine will; they viewed their arguments as opportunities to arrive closer to truth. They understood the active and sometimes heated exchange of ideas not as a source of division but just the opposite—an opportunity to create a shared conversation and a vision for the world as it ought to be.

Sadly, ours is an era of Korach, of cultural pugilism; self-interest dominates the common interest, and dialogue has devolved into a contact sport. The destruction of the Second Temple was caused not by geopolitics, idolatry, or immorality, but by the sin of *sinat ḥinam*, baseless hatred: the persistent human failing that allows minor differences of opinion to erupt into rancor and factionalism. We divide the world between us and them, fetishize our principles and demonize those of the other, while the temple around us collapses onto the idolatry of our own egos.

THE SIGNS OF this malady are evident for all to see. Long before the outrageous January 6, 2021, mob attacks on the United States Capitol, on one side of the political spectrum, uncomfortable truths are dismissed outright as fake and false. Better to reject anything we don't want to hear. Why enter the arena to debate ideas? Just shout down the other side with big lies and little lies, through television, through social media, through any megaphone that can drown out opposing views.

But the threat comes from the other side too. Our world is increasingly inhospitable to engaging any world-views different from our own. An uneasy uniformity of thought has become the norm in progressive circles, most sadly and most dangerously on university campuses, which are meant to be bastions of the active exchange of ideas. Speakers are disinvited, and students are self-censoring, disinclined to voice unpopular opinions for fear of being shouted down, canceled, and in some cases, threatened with physical violence. It is difficult enough to bear witness to the proliferation of book bans and other tactics of thought police in politically conservative communities; how much more so in communities once championing the banner of liberal discourse. The tactics may differ but the effects are the same: a narrowing of acceptable discourse, a retreat into an ideologically homogeneous echo chamber policed by the most recent orthodoxies of woke politics—all of which represent the most illiberal tendencies of all.

In the months following October 7th, I delivered a lecture on the contemporary Jewish experience at Cal State University, San Bernardino—the invitation to do so had been extended prior to October 7. The subject matter of my lecture was not political, but upon arriving on campus, I discovered that my presence was. A flyer announced that

I was a Zionist and, as such, a "genocide enabler," "actively involved in financing war crimes and crimes against humanity in Gaza." How, the flyer asked, could the university have invited a person like me to campus?

Neither the protesters nor their flyers (however inaccurate) really bothered me. What upset me, and—in all honesty—what saddened me was my exchange with students, following my remarks, or more precisely, my non-exchange with them. For every person asking me a question, there was a sidekick, phone in hand, recording my every word and move. It is a well-worn tactic of our times. An electronic ambush, a TikTok takedown or vigilante videography—the attempt to get a "hot-mic" moment that can then be clipped and posted to social media, sullying the character of the person caught in a "gotcha" moment.

I was ready and willing to talk to anyone—especially college students, especially students who hold views contrary to my own. But their insistence that they record everything was the telltale sign that their goal was not dialogue, but rather the performative leveraging of social media. I explained to the students that I would be happy to talk, to listen, and to debate, on the condition that they put their phones away. An exchange of ideas—by all means. A clip for their Instagram feed—no way. They refused, I declined to engage, and I walked away. It was all so very sad. An opportunity for dialogue and discourse, a chance to challenge someone's views and have my own views challenged, a chance to see that, despite our differences, we can dignify each other's humanity. A lost chance to build a bridge, a case study in the difference between arguments that are for the sake of heaven and those that are not.

Saddened as I am by such failed opportunities for dialogue with the "other" side, in our highly charged times, I am equally if not more pained when I see such "gotcha" aggressions among our own people. Individuals within the Jewish community do misrepresent the views of other individuals in public. People in positions of Jewish communal, journalistic, or rabbinic leadership who write a post or article maligning someone else, without even inquiring as to what that colleague said, and why. Debate—of course. Ad hominem attacks on the humanity of another—calling them "an enemy of the people," "self-hating," or "un-Jews"—no way. No matter where such individuals fall on the political spectrum, such behavior is reprehensible. It exists beyond the pale of civil discourse, a real-life example of *sinat ḥinam*. We should expect more from ourselves, and certainly from our leaders.

WITH THREATS COMING from all quarters, I believe we are living in a time when we have both the obligation and the opportunity, as a religious community, to remind the world of the importance of epistemic humility. *Epistemic* refers to anything dealing with knowledge; epistemic humility is a virtue, the quality of being humble in how we assert our knowledge. We need to remind people that truth is elusive, that admission of doubt is a sign of virtue, not weakness, and that listening, not speaking, is our greatest tool of communication. We need to remember the times in our life when we thought we knew it all, though now we know we didn't; someday in the not too distant future we may look back at the beliefs we hold today and have to make the same admission. We need to remind ourselves and the world that the force of our convictions is strengthened, not weakened, by engagement with views different than our own.

It might strike some as odd to hear a rabbi preach the importance of staying humble in speaking the truth. After all, isn't the job of religion to find certainty in uncertain times, to hear fundamental truths as mediated by scripture, prayer, and thundering sermons? In my mind, the point of religion, or at least good religion, is just the opposite: to teach us that, as much as we may think we know, there is far more in this world that we do not. Religious integrity lies less in the assertion that we possess the truth (which ultimately belongs to God and God alone) and more in the earnest search for truth, the never-ending aspiration to know the divine will, which, asymptotically, will always exist just beyond our reach. A teacher of mine once taught that the word *religion* has the root *lig,* as does *ligament,* something that connects two things. In religion, the connection is between humanity and the mysteries that remain elusive. To be religious is not to walk this earth with certainty. To be religious is to walk this earth filled with wonder, awe, and appreciation for what we don't know and may never know, but to remain, nevertheless, committed to seeking.

Our world is in desperate need of more, not fewer, religious people. The rabbis of the Talmud understood the active and sometimes heated exchange of ideas not as a source of division, but just the opposite: an opportunity to create arguments for the sake of heaven—a shared conversation and a vision for the world as it ought to be. Jewish sacred texts teach that truth is elusive and God's alone, that humility and a spirit of inquiry are acts of piety, and that every person is entitled to hold their opinions.

Epistemic humility is neither declaring ignorance nor ceding truth to another. It is not waving the white flag to relativism, surrendering that all truth is somehow shaped by context, so we can never really know anything. Epistemic humility is merely the virtue of knowing that a claim of truth must always be made with modesty, since human knowledge is necessarily incomplete. We never know anything fully, so when we do assert something, our proclamations of certainty should always be tempered with the tentative. Our assertions of truth may be best served by co-existing with the truths of another, even if theirs contradict our own. Epistemic humility is a demeanor, a posture that announces to the world that my right to be right does not preclude your right to be right. As individuals, as a nation, as citizens of the world, we are in desperate need of it.

ACCORDING TO TRADITION, the prophet of epistemic humility is Elijah—a figure whom we first encounter in the biblical book of Kings. A passion-filled prophet of the ninth century BCE, Elijah the Tishbite fought the good

fight, sometimes zealously so, the fight of monotheism opposing idolatry, in the northern kingdom of Israel, which
was then ruled by the wicked King Ahab and his Phoeni-
cian wife, Jezebel. Unlike most everyone else in history,
Elijah never dies, but instead is taken into the heavens in a
whirlwind, thus explaining his mysterious and peripatetic
presence at Passover seders, havdalah ceremonies, brises,
and other finely catered Jewish occasions. A redemptive
figure, Elijah is invited into our midst as spiritual protection at the liminal moments of our lives—when we transition from slavery to freedom (Passover), from the Sabbath
to the week ahead (havdalah), or when welcoming a baby
boy into the covenant of the Jewish people (bris). Elijah is
not just the most ubiquitous of all Jewish mystical figures,
but also the longest lasting—assigned to make his rounds
until the very end of time, when he will be the harbinger
of the Messiah.

So what does the biblical prophet Elijah have to do with
dispute resolution?

The Talmud is the foundational text of the Jewish people,
an anthology of rabbinic debate—the record of hundreds
of rabbis, over hundreds of years, arguing over just about
every topic, whether philosophical, theological, legal, or
practical. More often than not, the evidence, reasoning, or
stature of one sage takes precedence over that of his coun-
terpart in an argument. However, in some instances—319,
to be precise—the rabbis faced the two equally balanced
sides of an insoluble dispute, a debate to which they, in
a declaration of epistemic humility, conceded: it is something that will not be resolved until the end of times. In

such instances they declared "Teyku!," an acronym for *Tishbi y'taretz kushiot u-ba·ayot*; "the Tishbite"—meaning Elijah the Tishbite—will resolve difficulties and problems. (I wrote my doctoral thesis on a theologian, Rabbi Louis Jacobs, who wrote an entire book on the word *teyku*. My dissertation on Jacobs was titled—you guessed it—*Teyku*!)

To this day, in an Israeli soccer game, if the score is even at the end of the match, Israelis will not call it a tie, a draw, or a split; the word they will use is *teyku*. Off the athletic field, *"teyku"* has come to signal that the debate at hand will not be resolved until the end of times, when Elijah the Tishbite will reveal the answer. *Teyku*—a tie in this earthly realm—is an acknowledgment of the elusive nature of truth, the importance of epistemic humility, and the concession that not every debate will be resolved in our lifetime.

Elijah represents the possibility of a truth titrated over time, its power found not in top-down heavenly assertions but rather, like the butterfly that emerges from its cramped chrysalis, gently, humbly, and over time. Truth, as represented by Elijah, is neither singular nor sudden. It is modest, humble, and steady, able to hold its ground even as the world around it shakes.

The wounds caused by the divisions of our age bleed openly. Individuals unable to countenance politics different than their own; students whose minds are closed to engaging with uncomfortable ideas; brothers and sisters, members of the same family, unwilling to imagine a side of the story different than the one they have told themselves all these years. We do not need to give up our truths in order to hear others. We just need to learn to hold them humbly enough so that we can listen to other truths, which deserve an airing. This topic is more important than ever, following October 7th.

When will the prophet Elijah arrive? Nobody knows for sure. But tradition teaches that it will happen only when the hearts of parents are turned to their children, and the hearts of children to their parents (Malachi 3:23–24). In other words, when people soften their hearts and listen to the still, small voices seeking to be heard—that is when Elijah's presence will be felt. And on that day, *teyku*—the Tishbite will have arrived, and the Messiah will redeem us from our present sorrows.

PART THREE

What Might Be

TWELVE

THE DAY AFTER

Toward a Dialogue of Peace

Of all the ritual objects on the Passover seder table, one of the most well known is the Cup of Elijah. A pre-poured cup of wine awaits him at every seder—his arrival signaling not just Passover's freedom but also a future redemption and a "miracle" visit for every Jewish home. Growing up, I remember my father giving the table a nudge each year, smiling at us boys—the spilled wine a sign that Elijah had not only visited us but perhaps had enjoyed one sip too many.

With each passing year, new traditions were introduced to our seder table. Two in particular related to the Cup of Elijah. One year, a second cup, for the prophetess Miriam, was added, an inclusive nod to our biblical matriarchs alongside the patriarchs. The second is a custom whose origins are attributed to the Hasidic rabbi Naftali Tzvi of Ropshitz (1760–1817). Instead of pouring Elijah's cup at the beginning of the seder, an unfilled Elijah's cup is passed around the table. Each participant pours a bit of wine from their own cup into Elijah's as they share what they can do to bring about redemption. Sweet and simple as the custom is (it always left an impression on me, and it continues at my own seder table today), it is not enough to simply hope for a redemptive future. We are all obligated to do our part to fill Elijah's cup and thus contribute toward bringing about his arrival. We all play a part in making real our hoped-for future.

In the previous chapter, I noted the rabbinic connection between Elijah's arrival and the insoluble debates of Jewish tradition. As the prophet of epistemic humility, Elijah anticipates the hoped-for day when opposing sides can acknowledge the truth claims of the other, when contentious and sometimes toxic disagreements become arguments for the sake of heaven—as exemplified by the houses of Hillel and Shammai.

Now more than ever, each one of us must adopt the reconciliatory spirit of Elijah. The Jewish community suffers from the same culture of incivility as society at large. We are plagued by polarizing debates, ad hominem attacks, and the demonization of those whose views differ from our own. The disputes within the Jewish community today are not mere matters of ritual practice or theological belief. In a post–October 7th world, the arguments overflow in number and passion. How does Israel fight a just war in Gaza? How can Israel secure its own defense and the safety of the hostages, while minimizing the war's toll on Palestinian lives? Who should lead Israel into its next chapter? What role should America play? How should American Jewish institutions respond?

And underlying it all is perhaps the most contentious issue, the elephant in the room that informs so many other discussions—what Israelis call *yom aḥarei*, or "the day after." With the war still very much underway, it can feel unseemly to talk about, never mind debate, the future. And yet conversations about the long-term plan to resolve the Israeli-Palestinian conflict are both necessary and inevitable. The world is not waiting for the fighting to wane and all the hostages to be freed to discuss "the day after."

The US president has made clear his hopes for a two-state solution. Many in Israel, including its prime minister, have signaled that the establishment of a Palestinian state would only be a reward for terror. Amongst Israel's detractors are those who call for the removal of any Jewish presence "from the river to the sea"; and on both the Jewish and Palestinian sides, there are those advocating (albeit for different reasons) for some sort of binational one-state solution.

Few issues are as complicated and charged as the plan for "the day after"—a question that predates this moment yet whose urgency has been brought into clear relief in the present conflict. It is a conversation that is difficult to have in times of uneasy peace, all the more so to have today.

Which is why it is important to have that conversation and to conduct it in the spirit of Elijah. Prayers alone are not enough. Mirroring the spirit of Rabbi Naftali's seder custom, each one of us can contribute with an Elijah-like spirit of our own.

The question of how, in style and substance, to conduct a charged conversation is at the heart of resolving the Israeli-Palestinian conflict. It needs to be done in a manner that acknowledges and respects the hopes and fears of both sides. It means being Elijah-like—to take a posture of dialogue that judges generously, that refuses to demonize, and that affirms, even in the midst of differences, that neither side possesses the full truth.

Building on the previous one, this chapter is my modest contribution toward filling Elijah's redemptive cup—a "case study" of sorts, and a thought exercise.

THOSE WHO ADVOCATE a two-state solution have reasons that are historical, political, practical, moral, and Jewish. As the author and former peace negotiator Gidi Grinstein has pointed out, calls for a two-state solution are not new. Ever since the 1937 Peel Commission recommended partition, a broad international consensus has formed around some sort of Israel-Palestine land division. Every American president since Clinton has endorsed it, as have many Israeli prime ministers, including Ehud Barak, Ariel Sharon, Ehud Olmert, and Yair Lapid—even Benjamin Netanyahu did so at one time (as he stated in a 2009 speech at Bar Ilan University). However one feels about the thought of the United States recognizing Palestinian statehood, there is ample precedent: 193 countries have already done so.

A second reason is practical. Whatever your feelings about the Palestinians, if you are invested in the security of the Jewish state, the Palestinians must be given the opportunity and the burden of self-governance. As Harvard's former president Larry Summers once said, "In the history of the world, no one has ever washed a rented car." There is nothing—I repeat, nothing—that justifies the terror of October 7th, or any other terror, but common sense dictates that unless a people, Palestinian or otherwise, are given a path to self-rule, the cycle of violence will continue. Besides, as many have argued, Israel's present war can be considered just only insofar as it takes place alongside diplomacy. Netanyahu's half-baked postwar plan, his boasts of having stymied the two-state solution, and his finance minister's plan to harden the Jewish presence in the West Bank all undercut Israel's short- and long-term global standing and security.

Third, or third and fourth, are the moral and Jewish reasons. Israel's founding documents state the goal of being both a Jewish and democratic state. The present path to what some call "the one-state nonsolution" stands in opposition to those stated values. Math is math. Israel can be a Jewish state. Israel can be a democratic state. But it can't be both without a two-state solution. And as Jews, if the promise of Israel is founded on the right to be a free people in our own land, then how can we possibly deny another people that same right? As noted earlier, everyone deserves a place to call home. Nobody knows that better than Jews.

The reasons favoring a two-state solution are clear, strong, and compelling, but let's flip the argument for the sake of this exploration.

∽

THOSE WHO ADVOCATE against a two-state solution would say that calling for a Palestinian state is the delusional, self-soothing, shortsighted, and seductive siren song of liberal Jews who are oblivious to the harsh history, facts, and lived realities of the Middle East. Yes, there have been partition plans, two-state plans, and other plans for over a hundred years. What there hasn't been is a Palestinian peace partner willing to embrace Israel's right to exist.

The long history of Arab rejectionism (the 1937 Peel Commission, the 1947 UN Partition Plan, the 1967 Khartoum Resolution, and so on) betrays the truth: the root of the conflict is not some border dispute but the fact of Israel's existence itself. With chants like "We don't want no two states, we want all of '48" or "From the river to the sea, Palestine must be free," very little is left to the imagination. Whom, exactly, is Israel inviting to be its neighbors? History cuts both ways; two can play at that game.

So, too, one can argue that a two-state solution would be a reward for terror—a vindication of Hamas's strategy of October 7th. Those who call for a two-state solution are putting the carriage before the horse, having yet to figure out "small" details like the location of borders and capitals, systems of governance and security, Palestinian refugees, and the like. According to this view, October 7th revealed to the world the murderous intentions of a would-be Palestinian state. Why in the world would Israel be interested in establishing a "Hamastan" as its next-door neighbor? That autocratic entity would be poised to launch an endless series of Iran-supplied October 7ths, not just from Hamas in the south or Hezbollah in the north but right from the center of Israel, a stone's throw from major population centers.

Practically speaking, after October 7th, Israel is emotionally threadbare. There is zero trust in the Palestinians. The Israeli left is dead. If time will eventually be ripe for a full-court press on two states, now is positively not it. Save your lectures about Israel's standing in the international community. Last time anyone checked, there is no shortage of stateless people on this earth. The fact that the world is championing the Palestinians and not, say, the Kurds, the Rohingya, or the Uyghurs says more about the world's feelings toward the only Jewish state than it does about Israel.

As for the moral or Jewish argument, of course democracy is a value—a value, incidentally, not enjoyed by the Palestinians under present Hamas leadership or, presumably, in any future Palestinian state. So, given the choice between a less-than-democratic Israel and a Groundhog Day October 7th–filled future, I would take the former over the latter, as would any sensible person. I can also make an argument based on Jewish values and not just because, as many good Jews hold, Ma'aleh Adumim, Ariel, and Alon Shvut are just as much part of Israel as Tel Aviv, Beersheva, and Afula. The past two thousand years provide a case study in the price of Jewish vulnerability. The first priority of any state, especially the Jewish state, is the security of its citizenry, and it should be priority number one for the global Jewish people too. A two-state solution will bring neither peace nor security. It is time for liberal Zionists to move on.

∽

THE REASONS AGAINST a two-state solution are clear, strong, and compelling—as are the reasons for the two-state solution.

But this exploration was not about the merits of one side or another, so much as about the activity of debate. Point by point, we need to practice understanding without taking the argument personally. Every point has its counterpoint.

I am reminded of the rabbi who was asked to settle an argument between a husband and a wife. The rabbi listened to the wife, nodded his head, and said, "You're right." Then the husband stated his case, and the rabbi nodded his head and responded, "You're also right." The rabbi's intern, who had been there the whole time, blurted out, "But Rabbi, how can they both be right?" To which the rabbi responded, "You're right too!"

It is an old joke, but on a certain level it points to a fundamental role of religious leadership. Find a way to keep the conversation civil, to make sure both sides keep talking, even if, and especially if, they passionately disagree. In a world where the Jewish people do not lack for enemies, we dare not make enemies within our own ranks.

As for me—what do I believe? Well, not surprisingly—I do have an opinion—which is well known to everyone in my community. But more important than my personal views is my hope that the leadership that is modeled in my synagogue helps people to the left and right of me feel that they have a place. That their views have a place and that they can exchange their views respectfully.

I believe, based on all that I have seen and all that I have heard, that the time is not right for a top-down two-state solution (at least not in the spring of 2024, as I write this). Israel is in the midst of a war, there are hostages to be saved, we are traumatized. Everything is presently too raw; the time is not ripe.

And I believe, based on all that I have seen and all that I have heard, that the only path forward is a two-state solution. Not today and not tomorrow, but in a future that we can speak of openly and proudly, toward which we seed and fund ideas and initiatives, supporting all those leaders in Israel and America who are working toward such a vision and opposing those who don't. It is toward that future that we should gaze. Liberal Zionism—the belief in a Jewish and democratic state, and in two states for two peoples—may be on the wane, in decline, or even dead. But that doesn't mean it is not a noble and necessary idea to pursue.

To hold on to an ideal, to publicly affirm it, and to work toward it—even if its realization is not for the here and now—is not an easy position to take, and it contains, no question, a bit of inner contradiction. But then again, is it not the spirit that has impelled our people since our very beginning? What is the story of the wilderness wanderings if not the journey to a Promised Land, whether we get there or not? What is the vision of the prophets—Isaiah, Jeremiah, Ezekiel—if not the aspirational return from exile? What is the story of our past two thousand years, if not the tale of a people who, no matter what, through thick and thin, never lost hope? *Od lo avda tikvatenu* "Our hope is not yet lost," as the final stanza of Israel's national anthem, "Hatikvah," reminds us. There is nothing wrong, in fact, there is everything right, and everything Jewish, about staying true to an ideal, whether we realize it in our lifetime or not. When the time is ripe, may it be realized.

The arrival of a two-state solution, like the prophet Elijah himself, may not be imminent; but each of us can play a part in bringing it closer. Again, hopes and prayers are not enough. I am reminded of the sage rabbinic counsel: "If you have a sapling in your hand, and someone should say to you that the Messiah has come, stay and complete the planting, and then go to greet the Messiah" (Avot de Rabbi Nathan, 31b). We plant seeds today, even if the fruits are not to be enjoyed in our lifetime; each one of us personally contributes to the realization of a hoped-for redemptive vision to be shared by all.

It is not easy, then or now, to take a position that understands the diversity of voices at the Jewish table as part of the greater good. There will be potshots taken from the left and from the right. Sometimes a win will not be so much about advancing your own position, but in advancing the unity of the Jewish people. It is a strange thing to fight for, but today the Jewish world (and the world at large) desperately needs people and communities willing to proudly take such a stance.

I often return to a teaching of the late Rabbi David Hartman, a giant of twentieth-century Jewry and a lover of the people and the State of Israel. Rabbi Hartman was fond of citing a rabbinic text and used its punchline as the title of one of his books. The text describes the house of Hillel and the house of Shammai sharply disagreeing on matters of Jewish law, and the text asks: If the Torah is given by a single God, provided by a single shepherd, how is it the case that there exist such differing interpretations? And the answer given is this: "Make yourself a heart of many rooms and bring into it the words of the house of Shammai and the words of the house of Hillel." In other words, Hartman explained, a Jew must strive to be a "person in whom different opinions can reside together . . . who can feel religious conviction and passion without the need for simplicity and absolute certainty."

Here is the spirit that we need—whatever the future holds, in all the diversity of our views, we need to step forward together—we have hearts of many rooms. Not just the prophet Elijah, not just rabbis, but each and every one of us has the means to address the pathology of the hour; we must draw on the quiet heroism within us to contribute to this healing, this tikkun, of our hearts and our fractured world. If we can muster the courage to love one another as much as we love ourselves, if we can allow for the stakes to be higher than our own self-interest, and if we can approach the relationships dearest to us with humility and a deep desire for reconciliation—we can, each one of us and all of us together, mend this world.

THIRTEEN

THE
GENERATIONAL
DIVIDE

On Bridging the Politics of Zionism

Few parenting pleasures rank higher than the joy of taking one's daughter out to dinner with her friends. My wife and I did this when our oldest, Lucy, was spending her junior semester abroad in Copenhagen. Another young woman seated near me had, in a manner of speaking, grown up in my home. Over the years, I could walk into my kitchen at any time of night or day, to find her chatting away with my daughter Lucy, or, for that matter, with any of my children. I will call her Maya.

I was enjoying my meal when Maya turned to me. "Rabbi Cosgrove," she said, the formal address signaling that she was about to say something more significant than requesting another slice of pizza. "At Park Avenue Synagogue, do you have an Israeli flag on the pulpit?"

"Yes, Maya, we do," I replied.

"Do you recite the prayer for the State of Israel at Sabbath services?"

Maya was referring to the prayer, written in Hebrew shortly after Israel's establishment in 1948, that Jews pray to ask God to bring peace, counsel, and strength to the government and defense forces of Israel.

"Yes, Maya, we do recite the prayer for the State of Israel . . . You've been to services at Park Avenue Synagogue many times over the years. What is it you're really asking?"

Some time has passed, and the precise sequence of words that emerged from Maya's mouth remains a bit blurry—perhaps due to the beers we were drinking or to my surprise that the words were spoken at all—but it went something like this: "Rabbi, I think that national flags are political statements and that Zionism is a political ideology. You've always taught that Jews may be both an ethnic and religious group. But does my ethnicity have to be connected to nationality? Why do Jewish communities that claim to be politically unaffiliated have to support Zionism? What I see when I look at history is that nationalism has been used mainly to oppress and cause suffering. The Jewish people know this better than anyone else. Isn't it true that with the creation of the Jewish state, they became an oppressor to another group of people—the Palestinians? A Jewish nation-state, which by definition suffers from the same flaws and excesses of all nation-states, will never be able to uphold Jewish values. What I wanted to ask you is, haven't there always been non-Zionist Jews? It is important to me that there be successful non-Zionist Jewish examples and a place to practice Judaism and have a Jewish identity that do not involve supporting a nationalism which feels unjust, oppressive, and downright cruel."

Maya is as sharp as they come. She is warm, wonderful, and very, very funny. She is not just a proud Jew; she is a knowledgeable one. Her father is Israeli-born; her mother is a powerhouse in the Jewish community and sits on local and national Jewish boards. Maya is a product of Jewish day school, Jewish camping, and synagogue youth and Israel experiences; no small fortune has been invested in her Jewish identity—by her parents and by the Jewish community. And here she was, espousing a non-Zionist manifesto, a young woman who, I joke (this is no small point), shares a brain with my biological daughter, with whom she is very close.

Perhaps the shock I felt, the sense of being shaken, was partly the thought that if Maya felt this way, perhaps my Lucy did too, maybe not in the fully committed way that Maya was expressing, but enough to put distance between me and one of my children. Such a realization can be painful and disorienting, though of course inevitable. I was flabbergasted and, truth be told, flat-footed. I said nothing and the conversation pivoted to the pleasantries of the evening. I have since played the scene back in my mind. Was I right or wrong to hold my tongue as I did? It was meant to be a fun dinner for family and friends—hardly the time to have such a serious conversation.

The "Mayas" of the world are our future. Not just the future of Judaism but, more broadly, the future for all of us. In a post–October 7th world, it is more important than ever to engage in conversation with the Mayas around us and within us. All the feelings of tribalism and solidarity that I felt in the wake of October 7th do not reflect the feelings of these Mayas. Maya and her generation were skeptical about the proportionality of Israel's response to October 7th and its prosecution of the war. They had fundamental questions about the events leading to the attacks and the roles of nation-states. Truth be told, they were doubly alienated by the events of October 7th. Not only did they see Israel and Jewishness attacked, but they found themselves marginalized by the Jewish community that gave them life. And while one may be inclined to ignore these questions, dismissing them as the misguided ideas of youth, I believe that doing so is a profound error, both tactically and substantively.

Tactically, to ignore Maya's generation is to lose Maya's generation, and I care far too much about the Jewish future to do that. Substantively, I cannot dismiss her generation because intellectual honesty demands that I engage with ideas whether they align with my views or not. We are all, myself included, products of our time. My views are a reflection of my upbringing and influences, just as Maya's are a product of hers. I grew up in a time when support for Israel was part and parcel of the way I had formed my Jewish identity. We were still not much far removed from the Holocaust. Many of the teachers at my Hebrew school were Holocaust survivors; numbers were tattooed on their arms. The birth of the State of Israel—for them, and for me—was more than a miraculous culmination of an old multi-millennial dream. Israel was a stinging rebuke to what many believed to be the inescapable fate of the Jews: homelessness, persecution, and vulnerability.

I have long since played back what I would or should

have said to Maya. The exchange between us was not just about us, but about our generations. It raised questions about identity politics, the relationship of diaspora Jewry and Israel, and how, if at all, the chasm between the views of our different generations might be bridged.

Maya was giving expression to a Jewish identity untethered from the assumptions of my Jewish identity. Agree or disagree, she was operating from a place of authenticity and sincere intellectual inquiry. Any response to her position must therefore come from a place of generosity of spirit. What I heard from her (and from her generation) was that Israel represented a challenge to, not an expression of, her Jewish values.

How to respond to a non-Zionist Jewish Gen Zer? What should I have said? After much pondering and mulling, my response would go something like this:

Maya, first and foremost, I hear you. I hear you, your voice is important, and you are not alone. Judaism is not Zionism, and Zionism is not Judaism, and the flag on the pulpit and the prayer for Israel are complicated. There is indeed a long history of non-Zionist Jews, not self-hating Jews or messianists for whom the establishment of the State of Israel can happen only once the Messiah has arrived. Proud Jews: labor Zionists, cultural Zionists, even religious Zionists, Zionists who had attachments to the land but not to establishing a state. Big names like Mordecai Kaplan, who saw the Jewish people as a national civilization; Simon Rawidowicz, who believed in global Hebraism; and Hans Kohn, who had a vision of cultural humanism. For them, to be part of the Jewish nation was not about having a "state" per se, but about being attached to one another by way of folkways (Kaplan), the Hebrew language (Rawidowicz), and ethics (Kohn). When political Zionism began to take hold in the late 1800s, by way of Theodor Herzl's efforts, Orthodox and Reform Jews rejected it. In fact, the First Zionist Congress did not call for an actual state, but for a Jewish "national home, secured by public law"; it is not entirely clear what this vision entailed, but it is clear that Herzl did not have in mind organizing a military or creating borders or committing to many other trappings of statehood. Even a revisionist Zionist like Vladimir Jabotinsky, and even Israel's first prime minister, David Ben-Gurion, at different times in their lives had non-statist visions of the Jewish homeland. Until the Arab revolts of 1935, Ben-Gurion assumed Palestine would be a Jewish-Arab federation.

Maya, it pains me to say that there are some people— good people who are my friends and mentors—who would call you, for what you are saying, an "un-Jew." That by seeking a Jewish expression without a state, you are somehow no longer Jewish and have turned your back on the Jewish people. Those people should know better and should know their history better. Maya, not only are you not alone, not only are you a good Jew—but you stand in some very good Jewish company.

As someone of my generation, I can't imagine Judaism without Zionism, but I agree with you that Zionism is not Judaism. It is regrettable that to an overwhelming degree, the Jewish community in its religious and cultural institutions, and in its underlying attitude and assumptions, has made it seem so. When the State of Israel was founded in the wake of the Holocaust, the support of American Jewry was critical. If we weren't going to move to Israel, then we were going to support those who did—philanthropically and politically. Jews held fundraisers, started to lobby our government officials, and created a network of pro-Israel advocacy organizations, known by a vast alphabet soup of acronyms. Advocacy of Israel was embraced as a tool for solidarity, a response to antisemitism, and a prophylactic against assimilation. For Jews unfamiliar with the traditional language of Jewish ritual practice, this advocacy provides a civic form of Jewish practice. We have our slogans, we march in our parades, we buy Israel Bonds, we plant trees, and we write checks—acts important in themselves but also a rallying cry and bonding agent for American Jews. It didn't happen all at once, but yes, somewhere along the way American Zionism became, in the words of the late Rabbi Arthur Hertzberg, a "substitute religion." Even worse, it became a litmus test of loyalty to the Jewish community and cause. But as I said before, Zionism is not Judaism and Judaism is not Zionism, and we do both a disservice by confusing the two.

And yes, Maya, I also get it. When you look at Israel, when I look at Israel, when anyone looks at Israel, we see a state that sometimes stands in breach of many of our values, our Jewish values: democracy, religious pluralism, the Palestinian right to self-determination. How can I ask you to support an Israel that doesn't recognize you or support your fundamental beliefs? The math is not complicated. Fifty-two percent of young Israelis are either

Haredi or Arab; for them, non-Orthodox diaspora Jewry is an abstraction. A typical secular Israeli expends zero psychic energy thinking about the shared destiny of the Jewish people. Diaspora Jews do not help make Knesset coalitions, nor do we play a direct role in Knesset politics. Why exactly should you care about a place that does not acknowledge you, care about you, or even think about you?

Yet high on the list of Jewish values in the synagogue I lead, which has been part of your childhood and growing up, is love of Israel—whether or not Israel is lovable at any given moment. How should we manifest that love in the world? Yes, there is a strand of non-Zionist thought embedded in the Jewish "soul," and yes, the project of rabbinic Judaism took shape almost entirely outside the land of Israel; but it is, I believe, a profound misreading of Jewish history and the spirit that animates Judaism to call Judaism anything other than a land-centered faith. This has been the case since God's first call to Abraham—"to the land that I will show you"—to our arrival in the Promised Land, through the First and Second Commonwealths, through the exile, in the words of our prayers, the direction in which we pray, the rituals we observe, and the aspirations we hold, our eyes have always been turned toward Zion. Not just a shared faith, language, and culture, but an attachment to the land. Living there if you choose, and if you choose otherwise, supporting those who do. Supporting Israel is, in my mind, fundamental to what it means to be a Jew today. It is why we have the flag on my *bimah,* or synagogue pulpit, it is why we recite the prayer for Israel, it is why I am a proud Zionist, it is why I am politically

engaged on behalf of Israel, and why I ask that my congregants be as well, particularly now in our post–October 7th
world.

Does Israel's right to sovereignty clash with the Palestinians' same right? Of course it does. I often return to an
observation of the late Israeli iconoclastic thinker Yesha-
yahu Leibowitz; it is worth quoting in full:

> For the Jews . . . this country is the country of their
> people, even without any claim to "right," since
> no such counterclaim could deprive them of this
> [national] consciousness. But in the perverse course
> of history, which is incorrigible, an analogous bond
> was created between the same country and *another*
> nation. In their consciousness this country is theirs,
> whether their "right" to it is recognized or not.

Leibowitz's observation (made after the Yom Kippur
War) is so on point and painful to take in because it recognizes the impasse that any discussion of "rights" must come
to. No matter how many arguments are mustered, no matter how many times the history of the conflict is written
and rewritten—we will always return to the same starting
point. Two peoples with claims to the same piece of land.

Should Israelis, no different than the Palestinians, be
held responsible for their role in obstructing a two-state
solution? Absolutely. Israel is a deeply imperfect state that,
just like any nation-state, falls short of its stated values. But
Maya, given the choice between a sovereign and imperfect
Israel and the "moral purity" of exiled victimhood as lived

by our people for the two thousand years prior to 1948, I would choose the former over the latter any day.

And Maya, if you would deny your own people the right that you are willing to fight for on behalf of others, well, that is an act of self-abnegation that is more of a "you" problem than it is Israel's. Just because we acknowledge the right of another to hold a point of view different from our own doesn't mean we must abdicate our own right. I didn't choose to live during this historical era, in which a sovereign State of Israel exists, but I do. I am grateful that I do. Israel is the greatest achievement of the Jewish people over the past century, if not across the entirety of our existence—the expression of a multi-millennial hope, the home to half our people. I may not live there, but as long as I live, I will understand Israel as a constituent part of my Jewish being.

Today, Maya, Israel is not just troubled and troubling; Israel is on the brink. The fault lines have broken open before our very eyes: the future of Israel as a democracy, the outbreak of the October 7th War, and Israel's loss of standing in the community of nations. Could some of Israel's present predicament have been avoided? Is some of this pain self-inflicted? Absolutely. Notwithstanding the historical intransigence and violence of the Palestinians, could the organized Jewish community have been more forthcoming, cautioning Israel, as only an invested partner can, about the likely consequences of its policies? Of course. But let's stop living in the past and start asking what we do now.

There is a book by the late political economist Albert

Hirschman called *Exit, Voice, and Loyalty*. Hirschman explains that when a business, nation, or any human group is in crisis, there is a choice to be made. One can *exit*, meaning walk away, or one can have *voice*, meaning attempt to repair or change that relationship through grievance, engagement, or activism. No doubt it is easier to exit and avoid those "cumbrous political channels" that are the means to effect change. Some would say that to criticize Israel is a sign of disloyalty. I say otherwise. As always, there is the question of tact: our tradition warns us that our words and actions can be received and redirected in ways we never intended. We need to be careful that the critical words of those invested in Israel's success are not coopted as cover by those who seek Israel's failure. But just as my activism as an American is an expression of, and not counter to, my patriotism—so too my Zionism.

Israel is now in crisis. Are you going to exit—walk away and stand on the sidelines? Or are you going to use your voice—leverage your moral compass and the piercing clarity of your conscience to effect change, fight for your values, and help not only Israel but all the nations of the world realize a vision of national identity that does not oppress others? In Israel's case, given the ideals you champion, given the age you are, why on earth would you cede the discussion of what Zionism is and what it should be to those who are our people's true enemies or to your own Jewish kin who would corrupt Zionism, making it into something it is not and never should be? Encounter, T'ruah, Zionness, Seeds of Peace, Roots, Israel Policy Forum—there is no shortage of organizations fighting the good fight, and I know they would welcome your engagement.

Maya, let me end where I began. I hear you, your voice is important, and you are not alone. As your friend's father and as the rabbi of a synagogue, I am proud of you, and I am here for you. Not only do you have a place in the Zionist conversation, but also that conversation depends on you. We might not always agree, but make no mistake, now more than ever we need you, the larger Jewish community needs you, and Israel needs you.

FOURTEEN

THE BROKEN AND
THE WHOLE

*A New Vision of Zionism
and American Judaism*

History will remember October 7, 2023, as an inflection point. There will be a story of all that came before and all that came afterward. As I write this in April 2024, we remain very much in the shadow of October 7th—the war, the hostages, the unfolding humanitarian crises, the war's political and geopolitical ramifications in Israel, on college campuses across America, and around the globe.

The "post" of our post–October 7th reality continues to evolve. Our Israeli brothers and sisters struggle with how to prosecute war, secure peace, maintain the country's international standing, and address its internal divisions. So too American Jews face both new questions and old ones asked with new urgency. Questions related to our hyphenated identities, the invisible string that ties us to Israel, our sense of home in America. We told ourselves that we were different from the Jews of postwar Europe or ancient

Egypt or Persia. Now, after October 7th, we wonder if we have become but one more case study in the annals of the world's most ancient hatred. Our paradigms are shattered, and our eyes have been opened to a new reality. As we move forward, what stays and what goes? Is it time for a new script or time to double down on the old one?

In a world with no easy answers, I find both wisdom and comfort in a rabbinic midrash told of the darkest moments of biblical Israel's desert sojourn—the incident of the Golden Calf.

When Moses ascended Mount Sinai to receive the Ten Commandments, he stayed atop of the mountain for forty days and forty nights. The newly emancipated Children of Israel grew restless waiting for their leader to return and, needing something to worship, they built the Golden Calf.

When Moses descended the mountain and saw his people engaged in idolatry, he threw the tablets to the ground, shattering them. We know that a second set of tablets was constructed and placed in the Ark of the Covenant to accompany the Israelites on their journey forward. But what, the rabbis of the Talmud ask, happened to the shattered fragments of the first set? Were the shards left on top of the mountain? Perhaps, like the Golden Calf itself, they were destroyed—fragments of a painful memory better left in the past? Some things are best left behind.

The rabbis suggest otherwise. "Luchot ve'shivrey luchot munachim be'aron," states the Talmud. "The tablets and the broken tablets side-by-side in the ark together" (Berachot 8b). The image is powerful—both the broken and the whole lead Israel on the journey forward. We pick up the pieces. We remember the hurt, hold on to the pain, and nevertheless put one foot ahead of the other. Nothing is left behind. The forward momentum of our people actually depends on carrying both realities with us—shattered and whole, on our way to the Promised Land.

I believe the task of American Jewry is to find the means to bring both sets of tablets along on our journey ahead. We can integrate the wisdom of everything that came before October 7th, the newly learned wisdom of our post–October 7th reality, and most of all, the fact that the truth is not present exclusively in one or the other but in the integration of the two. A new vision for American Judaism and American Zionism, the shattered truths we held sacred and a bold new vision that embraces the complexity, paradoxes, and even the internal contradictions of our time. Our engagement with Israel, our engagement with tradition, and perhaps most of all, our engagement with one another will lend us support.

So what should American Zionism look like, moving forward?

First and foremost, we need an American Zionism that begins with love for the Jewish people and teaches our children and grandchildren the story of our exile, the pitfalls of powerlessness, the dreams of every wave and every stage of our national longings, and our right to the land. American Jewry has become woefully ahistorical. We need a "Marshall Plan" to rebuild our deficit of memory; you can't love a country that you know only by way of social media. We need formal, informal, and most important, experiential curriculum; our children should be in dialogue with Israeli children by way of technology, exchange programs, sister congregations, any means available. We need Israel educators, "reverse" Birthright programs bringing Israelis into contact with American Jews, and a redoubling of efforts on teaching the Hebrew language—perhaps our people's most effective bridge to one another, to our past, and to our future. We need to do more, we need to do it better, and we need to be all in.

Next, we need an American Zionism with a dose of humility. The Middle East is not New York City, and the democratically elected government of Israel has every right to make decisions in the best interests of Israel, even when these decisions run contrary to our sensibilities. Israel lives in a very rough neighborhood, and the community of nations holds Israel to a nasty double standard that is often, but not always, laced with explicit or implicit antisemitism. Lest we forget, Abraham was called *ha-ivri,* meaning "the other," because he stood alone when the rest of the world stood on the other side. There is nothing wrong, in fact there is everything right, about standing at Israel's side, even when, and sometimes especially when, it makes decisions we ourselves would not make. In school, on campus, and on Capitol Hill, the coming generation of American Zionists must be given tools that will help them be resilient, self-confident, and adroit defenders of the real, not the imagined, Jewish state.

But for the next chapter of American Zionism to ring true and stand the test of time, we must also be willing and able to integrate the universal and prophetic dimension of American Jewry. If the project of Zionism, as Martin

Buber once reflected, is the Jewish use of power tempered by morality, it is a project that sometimes Israel gets right and sometimes gets wrong. If the dream of Israel is to serve as a homeland for all Jews and all forms of Jewish expression, we must confront the bitter truth that this dream is now threatened by the government of the Jewish state. There is bitter irony in the realization that, because of the stranglehold of the ultra-Orthodox Chief Rabbinate, many Jews cannot practice their Judaism freely in the Jewish state. As evidenced by political infighting and the judicial reform protests prior to October 7th, Israel faces this challenge: how to remain a liberal democracy without giving short shrift to security concerns. There is nothing wrong with helping, chiding, or goading Israel toward achieving this complicated goal, as long as that nudging comes from a place of abiding concern for Israel's safety and security. The "sane center" must not let those who have embraced the ideological and philanthropic extremes define the field of play and terms of debate. We who live between the forty-yard lines have a unique role to play in American Zionism today. We can support religious pluralism, efforts to achieve Arab-Jewish coexistence and dialogue, and constructive steps toward creating a two-state solution. Because the stakes are so high, the sane center must speak—with passion and with volume. We must protect each other from the ideologues on the extremes, rallying men, women, money, and discipline for a cause that is just. Above all, we must let the Jewish world know that we are all in this together.

Finally, we need to understand that the new American

Zionism is not a substitute for American Judaism. For far too many Jews, support for Israel became a vicarious faith, a civil religion masking the inadequacies of our actual religion. The only way Israel will learn from, listen to, or care about American Jews is if we show ourselves to be living energetic Jewish lives. To be good Zionists, we must be better Jews. A robust American Jewish identity can weather policy differences with this or that Israeli government and withstand the indignity of being a punching bag for a campus culture run amok—something a paper-thin Jewish identity cannot do.

Build up your own Jewish identity and that of your children and grandchildren, and do everything in your power to support individuals and institutions committed to nurturing and sustaining the global Jewish community.

Taking agency over our Jewish lives was a lesson instilled in me early on. Here's an example from my own life. Grateful as I am for my Jewish identity growing up, when I went off to college at the University of Michigan and encountered the freedoms of campus living, I wasn't terribly involved in Jewish life. One Friday afternoon of my junior year, my parents called to tell me that Mr. Gendon, a grandfatherly figure whom I sat next to in synagogue while growing up, had died. Not really knowing what to do, but knowing I had to do something, I decided to go to the Friday night service at Hillel to say kaddish. I told my friends that I would be a bit late for our usual Friday night outing, and off I went.

I knew no one at Hillel. I had been there only on the High Holy Days. I sat through the Friday night service, and

I said kaddish for Mr. Gendon. When it was over, as if I had arrived at the end of a long flight, I jumped up and headed straight for the exit. When I was almost home free, a man blocked my escape route. "Excuse me," he said. "I notice you've never been here before. I was wondering if you have plans for Shabbat dinner."

Truth be told, I lied. Figuring he didn't want to hear about "Dollar Pitcher Night" at the local bar, I said that I did have plans. He then said something that I will never forget—it changed my life forever.

"Well, I bet you don't have plans for next Friday night!"

I shrugged sheepishly.

"Good," he said. "So I will see you then."

The following week I went back to services and Shabbat dinner. I went again and again, became a Hillel board member, led a pro-Israel group to Washington, DC, edited the Jewish student journal, went to Israel, went to rabbinical school, got a doctorate in Jewish history, and—to make a long story short—became who I am today.

Of the million lessons from that single exchange, I return to two.

First: The man who stood between me and the exit that day was Michael Brooks, then the Hillel director at the University of Michigan. Aside from having built a campus Hillel that was a national model, he set an example of personal leadership that remains the bar to which I continue to aspire. The ability of one person to change the life of another, of one soul to seek the spark in another—that is the tried-and-true means by which to secure the Jewish future.

Second: We must take agency in our Jewish lives. To be born Jewish is an accident of history. Given the freedoms of America, living Jewishly is a choice, an identity that can be shed without cost or consequence. The challenges of our moment are enough to prompt a Jew on the periphery to choose the easier path of disaffiliation, inertia, and apathy. In college, positive as my points of Jewish identification were, it was not an identity that traveled with me—Judaism was something I "did at home." But on that otherwise nondescript Friday night, my Jewish identity was reborn and remade as an active choice to live Jewishly each and every day of my life.

Taking agency in our Jewish lives—this is the North Star of my vocation as a rabbi. Not everyone will choose to be a rabbi. But the choice to take agency is something we all must face—be it Esther in the house of Ahasuerus, me at Hillel, or any person asking whether to lean into the opportunity and blessing of being connected to a tradition, people, and faith.

The future of American Zionism is contingent on the future of American Judaism—not the other way around. American Jewry must redouble its investment in Jewish life and living. As invested as we are in Israel, for the sake of our Jewish and Zionist future we must prioritize efforts to cultivate rich Jewish identities: synagogues, schools, and Jewish summer camps filled with Jews living intentionally and joyfully, capable of producing the next generation of American Judaism and training of the next generation of rabbis, cantors, Jewish educators, and professionals.

An American Zionism filled with love, humility, and

intentional Jewish living will not be monolithic. It must be sufficiently supple and capacious to house many voices. Can an American Jew emphatically support Israel's right to self-defense and self-determination and yet be critical of the Israeli government? Can that person be vigilant on Israel's behalf and empathetic on the Palestinians' behalf? For far too long, American Jewry has been fed a series of binaries, a choice between one or the other only.

Such a narrow range of options must be called out as false; in a new American Zionism, it must be rejected outright. We who love Israel can be both critical and supportive of Israel. The hundreds of thousands of Israelis at the forefront of the protest against judicial reform became Israel's most capable defenders following October 7th. So too those American Jews who spoke out against Israel's government and on behalf of Israeli democracy prior to October 7th, myself included. We have now pivoted, unflinching in our support for Israel. In American Jewry's support of a Jewish and democratic State of Israel, criticism and love are not in opposition—they are two sides of the same coin. It is not either/or. I am reminded of David Ben-Gurion's comment after the outbreak of war in 1939, as the British issued the infamous White Paper restricting Jewish immigration to pre-state Palestine. "We will fight the White Paper as if there is no war and fight the war as if there is no White Paper." We, who love Israel as we do, must support Israel even as we harbor objections to the Israeli government.

As American Jews witness the precipitous rise of anti-Israel sentiment and antisemitism today, should we be self-reflective or reach out? The answer is not one or the other—it is both. As we find ourselves at odds with many educational, cultural, and political institutions—should we recuse ourselves or rescue these institutions from within? The answer is not one or the other—it is both. Must American Jewry steadfastly advocate for Israel's right to self-defense or express empathy for Palestinians, who are pawns in the inhuman strategy of Hamas? The answer is not one or the other—it is both. As we face a cross-generational schism concerning our obligations to Israel, American Jewry must construct a big tent capable of housing a plurality of voices. At all costs, our culture of debate must avoid the enemy within—baseless hatred, *sinat ḥinam*—in the form of ad hominem attacks intended to "cancel" others rather than focus on issues. The choice is never between empathy or vigilance, security or peace; much can be gained—new ideas, new insights—by placing these values in dialogue.

In his eulogy for the late Shimon Peres, Prime Minister Netanyahu spoke of the differences between them, reflecting on one late-night conversation in particular:

"From Israel's perspective," Netanyahu asked Peres, "what is paramount: *bitaḥon*, security, or *shalom*, peace?"

Shimon replied, "Bibi, peace is the true security. If there will be peace, there will be security."

Bibi responded, "Shimon, in the Middle East, security is essential for achieving peace and for maintaining it."

The debate intensified, the two men argued, one from the left, the other from the right, one the prophet of peace and the other the protector of Israel, until, like two worn-out prizefighters, they put down their gloves. So, who was right? With the passage of time, Netanyahu reflected on their exchange, concluding *sh'neinu tzodkim*, "we are both right." Though their politics differed, Netanyahu explained, no one camp has a monopoly on truth, and their views stemmed from a shared and principled commitment to Israel's future. In Netanyahu's words: "The goal is to ensure our national existence and coexistence. To promote progress, prosperity, and peace—for us, for the nations of the region, and for our Palestinian neighbors."

Not just the competing visions, but the manner by which those visions are negotiated—that is the task Israel faces, and American Jews have a critical role to play in shaping what will be. It is not easy to balance the binaries, especially when the stakes are high—but as a people, binaries are at the essence of who we are. F. Scott Fitzgerald once reflected that "the test of a first-rate intelligence is the ability to hold two opposed ideas in the mind at the same time, and still retain the ability to function." After October 7th, it might be said that the test of a first-rate Jew is the ability to hold two *ideals* at one and the same time.

The twentieth-century scholar Simon Rawidowicz wrote a now-famous essay titled "Israel: The Ever-Dying People." In it he explains the belief held in every age and stage of Jewish existence: surely this one was to be the last one. From Abraham to Rabbi Akiva, from Shushan to the former Soviet Union—whether because of persecution, dispersion, or the forces of assimilation, we are a people marked by the perennial belief that we are at risk of extinction. Then, of course, the next generation arrives—

utterly convinced of the same idea. Rawidowicz argues that our multi-millennial against-the-odds survival as a people is not based on anxiety about this notion; rather, every generation has leveraged this mentality to respond and act, leading us from strength to strength and building bridges from one Jewish generation to the next. Like Queen Esther on that fateful night, we did not surrender to fear and dread, and we lived to see another day.

And now our generation has its opportunity to respond to this idea, our people's recurring cri de coeur concerning its survival.

The late Maya Angelou wrote that "courage is the most important of all the virtues, because without courage you can't practice any other virtue consistently." As a people, our faith is directed not just toward God or one another. Our faith is a combination of courage and hope wrought from within, which impels us to work feverishly toward a bright Jewish future. We are not unaware of the hurdles we face or the possibility of failure. We carry both sets of tablets with us. That which is broken and that which is whole lead us on our journey to the Promised Land, forging for ourselves and others a better life and a better world.

FIFTEEN

TO BEGIN AGAIN

Stepping Toward the Promised Land

In my twenty-five years as a rabbi, no one I have coun-
seled through the Jewish stages of mourning has ever
shared that they have "gotten over" the loss of a loved one.
At best, the ritualized phases help us put one foot in front
of the other, to remember the people who have died even
while we look toward the future with hope.

Since the horrific attacks of October 7th, time and again
I have returned to these ritualized stages in search of a scaffolding that will help us make sense of our loss.

We start with *aninut*—the period between death and
burial, when words fail. We do not recite the kaddish
prayer prior to burial nor formally receive visitors. Accli-
mating to the painful new reality of loss and making prepa-
rations for the service and mourning process are done at
this stage, and little else.

Next, we sit *shiva*—the seven days of mourning following burial. Here we accept condolence visits and words of
consolation and begin to share memories of the deceased.
We come together for *minyan*, and community members
offer comforting words of sympathy. Only on the seventh

day do we "get up" from *shiva* to resume any semblance of daily life.

Shloshim lasts thirty days. We return to work, school, or another basic daily routine but still avoid non-essential socializing and entertainment. Finally, there is a year of *avelut*, a somber period in which we continue to say the mourners' kaddish for parents, often culminating with the unveiling of a memorial headstone. Our loved one's *yahrzeit*, the annual day of remembrance, will be observed into the years to come.

The rites and rituals of Jewish mourning provide us the tools to journey through the emotional phases of loss—from shock, to anger, to grief, and eventually to acceptance and a return to life, not as it was before, but a changed life, absent that loved one. These rituals do not take pain away. We just move through them—figuring out how to put one foot in front of the other. We remember, but we step forward. The ache remains, but we nevertheless plan for the future.

The Jewish people today are experiencing intense grief and grieving, moving from stage to stage, though the phases may blur together. The analogy is far from perfect. The passing of a beloved relative happens on a certain day; but because hostilities continue, daily sacrifices of civilians and soldiers continue to occur, and hostages, whose condition remains unknown, are still held captive by Hamas. The sorrows of the present are still unfolding—the traumas not yet fully known. The cascade of October 7th is still rippling through Israel and the world. Hence, the mourning process overruns the familiar rituals of Jewish mourning.

As for the *yahrzeit*—among all the cruelties of the October 7th attacks, it is particularly painful that they were perpetrated on one of the most joyous days of the Jewish year, Simchat Torah ("The Joy of Torah"). Simchat Torah marks the renewal of the Jewish people's annual cycle of scriptural reading—from Genesis to Deuteronomy and back to the beginning. Whatever the State of Israel may decide in regard to public commemorations, in the years to come, the *yahrzeit,* the memorial observance of the attacks, will fall not on the secular date of October 7 but on the Hebrew date of Simchat Torah. A joyous day will now be forever associated with memorial observances.

Difficult as the thought of kaddish-filled Simchat Torahs may be, we find wisdom and perhaps a touch of comfort at the intermingling of the themes of remembrance and renewal, grief and hope for the future. Long before October 7th, Simchat Torah focused on both loss and new beginnings. The ritualized renewal of the Torah, as set forth by the rabbis, asks that we read of the death of Moses in the final verses of the book of Deuteronomy in the same sitting where we open up to the creation of the world as found in the first verses of Genesis. Endings and beginnings—at one and the same time.

To begin again: this is the spiritual DNA of our people. As Jews, when we open the Bible, we focus not so much on what Adam and Eve did or did not do in the garden, but rather on their ability to reconstitute their lives following their brief stay there. The first couple, made painfully aware of the limitations of their own mortality, extend the reach of their existence by bringing children into this world. As the Holocaust survivor Elie Wiesel famously wrote: "According to Jewish tradition, creation did not end with man, it began with him. When He created man, God gave him a secret—and that secret was not how to begin, but how to begin again."

Many of our people's stories are about new beginnings—individuals, families, and sometimes an entire nation proved capable of carving a path forward after loss. Noah plants a vineyard following the devastating destruction of the flood. Abraham and Sarah journey to Canaan after the death of Abraham's father, Terah, and a lifelong struggle with infertility. Isaac makes sense of his life again after the singular experience of nearly becoming a sacrifice on an altar. Jacob seeks to rebuild his life on his own terms, in a new land, after fleeing his brother, Esau, and his household of origin. Joseph rises up to save himself, his adopted homeland of Egypt, and his brothers—the ones who had thrown him into a pit and sold him into slavery. These people, these great patriarchs and matriarchs, are our heroes. Like the Israelites as they crossed the sea into freedom, these exemplars found the strength to integrate their sorrow into a vision for a brighter future.

By a certain telling, this ability to see life anew in the face of sorrow is an aspect of being a human created in the image of the divine. A favorite rabbinic midrash of mine offers the extraordinary thought that even God had to find the spiritual wherewithal to begin anew. The midrash explains that God created and destroyed not one, not two, but a thousand worlds before settling on the one in which we currently live, with all its imperfections. And if God had to cultivate resilience, how much more must we. We will learn to rise up from sorrow. To hurt is human, to begin again is divine.

From our biblical forebears, to the prophet Jeremiah's command to rebuild following exile, to the establishment of rabbinic Judaism following the destruction of the Temple, to the founding of the State of Israel in the wake of the Shoah—this is the fundamental DNA of our people.

The question facing the Jewish people today is not how to begin, but how to begin again. I grieve over the victims of October 7th. I think of the Israeli soldiers fighting for Israel's security in Gaza. I think of the Gazan civilians caught in the crossfire of war. I grieve over the loss of innocent Palestinian lives—not to do so would be inhuman. Most of all, I shed tears when I consider the endless and compounding cycles of generational violence. Knowing how I feel, I am doubly sure that this is a feeling that I do not want to last for the rest of my life and into the lives of my children and grandchildren.

In mourning we find that path forward even as we remember the hurt, the pain of the loss. This grief can only be managed, never transcended. We must nonetheless consider the future, build a new vocabulary to help us work toward it and ultimately realize it, and, as our tradition teaches, honor the dead by choosing life. Our love of Israel and humanity demands that we bring an end to the cycle of generational violence, for the sake of our children and grandchildren.

At the conclusion of every Jewish wedding, we invoke the precarious condition of the Jewish people. Often a melody is sung, reminding all present that even at the height of our joy, we keep in mind the shattered condition of our people:

> If I forget thee O Jerusalem, let my right-hand
> wither, let my tongue cleave to my palate if I
> cease to think of you, if I do not keep Jerusalem in
> memory even at my happiest hour.
>
> *(Psalm 137:5-6)*

The final act of a Jewish wedding ritualizes this passage from Psalms, the shattering of a glass beneath the feet of the bride and groom. Even and especially as we set our sights to the future with joy, we make space for the pain of our people.

In the many weddings at which I have officiated since October 7th, I have found my thoughts lingering on this well-known Jewish ritual—always powerful—more so now. The shards beneath the wedding canopy represent the Jewish people, broken apart and scattered. And yet, like the wedding couple taking their first step into the future by way of those shards, so too must we. Holding pain, even as we dream of brighter times—ready to begin, and begin again. Remembering the hurt, but nevertheless putting one foot ahead of the other. It is not everything, but it is a place to start. And God knows, we are all in need of a place to start. Wholeness and brokenness, every step of the way, on our journey toward the Promised Land.

ACKNOWLEDGMENTS

A rabbi's success is measured not merely in their ability to impart faith in his or her parishioners. Twenty-five years into my rabbinate, it is clear to me that the success of any rabbi is based on the willingness of others to place their faith in him or her. A rabbi is only a rabbi insofar as people believe in that rabbi's ability to preach, teach, lead, and pastor to meet their spiritual needs and aspirations. As the old quip goes: "A leader without followers is just a person taking a walk."

This book represents a whole lot of people who believed in me.

For many years, my agent, Jennifer Weis, believed that I had "a book in me." With her coaxing, nudging, and counseling, I could not ask for a better advocate and sounding board.

Thank you to Sarah Pelz at Harvest / HarperCollins for believing in the need for a book on Jewish identity in a post–October 7th world and entrusting me with the opportunity to produce it. Writing, editing, publishing, and publicizing a book on a compressed timeline takes professionalism, patience, and, most of all—a sense of humor. Sarah, Emma Effinger, Lisa Glover, Abigail Marks, Sharyn Rosenblum, Katie Tull, and the entire team have been steadfast in their efforts, and I am grateful beyond words.

I am grateful to Ken Wapner, my writing sherpa and editorial counsel and coach. The writing of this book, both its subject matter and pace, has been intense, and I can say with absolute surety that it would not have happened without Ken's vision, good humor, encouragement, and demand for excellence.

I am indebted to a handful of trusted individuals including Adam Ferziger, Aiden Pink, Rebecca Raphael, and Jodi Rudoren, who graciously read elements of the manuscript as it was taking shape. Particular gratitude goes to Marga Hirsch who has an unparalleled familiarity with *The Chicago Manual of Style* and my writing. A special thank-you to Sam Truitt for masterfully assembling the endnotes. All errors are, of course, the responsibility of my mother.

Thank you to the editorial leadership of *Sapir* for granting permission to reproduce elements of an earlier article, "Continuity Requires Religion" (Autumn 2021).

More than any single individual, it is the faith the congregational family of Park Avenue Synagogue has placed in me as their rabbi that has sustained my efforts. Park Avenue is a community in which national Jewish conversations are lived, and its members inspire me each and every day. I am particularly grateful to my colleagues—the finest team of synagogue professionals ever assembled, whose commitment to Jewish life and collegiality make coming to work a daily blessing. In particular, I thank Lesley Alpert-Schuldenfrei, Rabbi Lori Koffman, Cantor Mira Davis, Valerie Russo, Cantor Azi Schwartz, Rabbi Bradley Solmsen, Rabbi Shayna Zauzmer, Susan Zuckerman, and my dear friend and wingman—Rabbi Neil Zuckerman.

The magic of Park Avenue Synagogue comes by way of a trusted group of lay leaders—officers and board members whose trust in the synagogue professionals, myself included, make everything possible. As chairmen over the years, Alan Levine, Geoff Colvin, Amy Bressman, Steve Friedman, Art Penn, and the boards they represent have built a thriving vision of Jewish life and provided me and my colleagues a playground to dream of the endless possibilities for synagogue life. So too the friendship and support of Menachem Rosensaft, Brian Lustbader, Paul Corwin of blessed memory, Natalie Barth, and Lizzy Markus have sustained me every step of the way. Particular thanks go to the present chairman, Mark First, whose personal and professional encouragement to write this book has made all the difference. My past chairman and dear friend Marc Becker, of blessed memory, taught me so many things, most of all, to make every day count. In no small way the writing of this book is a tribute to Marc's legacy, our friendship, and his deep love for Israel, our synagogue, and the Jewish people.

To Andrea and Ivan Lustig, Julian Zelizer and Meg Jacobs, and Lori and Brett Zbar—thank you for your love and encouragement.

The reader of this book will hopefully sense how important my family has been to shaping my identity. My close relationships with my siblings, siblings-in-law, and parents-in-law are what makes this journey through life fun, and I am grateful to each of you and all of you for more than can be put into words.

My children, Lucy, Maddie, Zoe, and Jed, are now outstanding young adults with thoughts and opinions of their own. I am so proud of each of you and there is literally nothing in life that makes me happier than the love you share with each other. If this book succeeds in setting the tone for an intergenerational dialogue on contemporary Jewish life and diaspora-Israel relations, it will be because it was written with you in mind.

To my wife and love of my life, Debbie. You are the best thing that has ever happened to me.

My parents, Gabrielle and Malcolm Cosgrove, have believed in me since my very first breath. The home you created for your sons, the values you instilled in us, and the confidence you gave us to set out on life's journey are gifts that can never be repaid. I am grateful to you for believing in me and dedicate this book in your honor. I love you both very much.

NOTES

Introduction

xxi *"Amazing / How everything"*: Michael Zats, "Illusion," https://
    images.shulcloud.com/1367/uploads/Documents/Website
    /KorazimPoemsforthesedaysOctober2023.pdf.

xxv *constituted by a mélange:* Shmuel Rosner and Camil Fuchs,
    #IsraeliJudaism: Portrait of a Cultural Revolution (Jerusalem: The Jewish
    People Policy Institute, 2019).

1. Living the Hyphen

6 *"the Jew resides":* Paul Mendes-Flohr, *German Jews: A Dual Identity*
    (New Haven and London: Yale University Press, 1999), 44.

6 *"two souls, two thoughts":* W.E.B. Du Bois, *The Souls of Black Folk*
    (Boston: Bedford Books, 1997), 38.

7 *"who live within":* Rabbi Abraham Joshua Heschel, *The Insecurity
    of Freedom: Essays on Human Existence* (New York: Farrar, Straus and
    Giroux, 1966), 197.

8 *first an American:* Dan Elbaum, "Why Golda Still Matters,"
    Philadelphia Jewish Exponent, August 23, 2023, https://www.jewish
    exponent.com/why-golda-still-matters/.

8 *"Once I thought":* Oscar Handlin, *The Uprooted: The Epic Story of the
    Great Migrations That Made the American People* (Philadelphia: University
    of Pennsylvania Press, 1951), 3.

8 *cultural assimilation:* Israel Zangwill, *The Melting-Pot: Drama in
    Four Acts* (New York: Macmillan Company, 1909).

9 *his utopian vision:* Maurice Wohlgelernter, *Israel Zangwill: A Study*
    (New York: Columbia University Press, 1965), 21–30.

9 *"every type of instrument":* Horace M. Kallen, *Culture and Democracy in the
    United States* (New York: Boni and Liveright Publishers, 1924), 124.

9 *decades to come:* Horace Kallen, "Democracy Versus the Melting-Pot:
    A Study in American Nationality," *The Nation*, February 25, 1915.

10 *"Marranos in reverse":* Eugene Borowitz, *The Mask Jews Wear: The
    Self-Deceptions of American Jewry* (New York: Simon & Schuster,
    1973), 10.

10 *"What is good for":* Salo W. Baron, *A Social and Religious History of the Jews*
    (New York: Columbia University Press, 1960), 3.

2. The Invisible Thread

18   *"My heart is in the east":* Judah Halevi, "My Heart Is in the East,"
      Zionism and Israel on the Web, http://www.zionismontheweb.org
      /yehudalevi.htm/.

19   *"One campaigns in poetry":* Sandy Levinson, "Bernie Sanders's
      Intellectual Sleight-of-Hand," *Balkinization*, February 27, 2020,
      https://balkin.blogspot.com/2020/02/bernie-sanderss-intellectual
      -sleight-of.html.

20   *Ben-Gurion would make clear:* Simon Rawidowicz, *State of Israel,
      Diaspora and Jewish Continuity: Essays on the "Ever-Dying People"* (Chicago:
      University of Chicago Press, 1998), 194.

23   *would not attempt:* Amanda Borschel-Dan, "Abrasive Israel,
      Apathetic Diaspora Behind Jewry's Widening Gap, Says Report," *Times
      of Israel*, June 28, 2018, https://www.timesofisrael.com/abrasive
      -israel-apathetic-diaspora-behind-jewrys-widening-gap-says-report/.

23   *"Israel will continue":* Charles S. Liebman, "Diaspora Influence
      on Israel: The Ben-Gurion Blaustein 'Exchange' and Its Aftermath,"
      Jewish Social Studies, vol. 36, nos. 3–4 (July–October 1974), 278.

23   *"pushed too hard":* David Horowitz, ed., *Yitzhak Rabin: Soldier of Peace*,
      (London: Halban Publishers, 1996), 188.

26   *"I could be you":* Nathan Guttman, "Yair Lapid's Great American
      Tour," *Forward*, October 11, 2013, https://forward.com/opinion
      /185425/yair-lapids-great-american-tour/.

3. The Two Worlds of Judaism

32   *ingathering of Jewish exiles:* "The Declaration of the Establishment
      of the State of Israel," Ministry of Foreign Affairs, May 14,
      1948, https://www.gov.il/en/pages/declaration-of-establishment
      -state-of-israel.

33   *"lived with":* Einat Wilf, "Choosing Our Allies," AJC *Global Voice*,
      June 3, 2018, https://www.ajc.org/news/choosing-our-allies.

37   *"the bargain of":* Jacob Katz, "Emancipation and Jewish Studies,"
      Commentary, April 1974, https://www.commentary.org/articles
      /jacob-katz/emancipation-and-jewish-studies/.

40   *"The lack of support":* Gil Troy, *The Zionist Ideas: Visions for the Jewish
      Homeland: Then, Now, Tomorrow* (Philadelphia: Jewish Publication
      Society, 2018), 295–96.

46   *"everything that touches":* Rainer Maria Rilke, "Love Song," *Poem-a-Day*
      (Academy of American Poets), April 4, 2021, https://poets.org
      /poem/love-song-0.

NOTES

209

4. Empathy and Vigilance

53 *"This wonderful old"*: Isidore Wartski and Rev Arthur Saul Super, *The Children's Haggadah* (London: Routledge & Kegan Paul, 1963), 11.

56 *"We used to take"*: Hebrew Immigrant Aid Society and *Vox*, September 26, 2015, https://hias.org/news/we-used-to-take-refugees-because-they-were-jewish-now-we-take-them-because-were-jewish-vox/.

58 *European antisemitism:* Theodor Herzl, *The Jewish State* (New York: Dover Publications, 1989).

58 *their own destiny:* Leon Pinsker, *Auto-Emancipation: An Appeal to His People by a Russian Jew* (1882), Jewish Virtual Library, https://www.jewishvirtuallibrary.org/quot-the-jewish-state-quot-theodor-herzl.

58 *"House of Jacob"*: "Texts Concerning Zionism: BILU Manifesto (1882)," Jewish Virtual Library, https://www.jewishvirtuallibrary.org/bilu-manifesto.

59 *Jewish helplessness:* Chaim Nahman Bialik, "The City of Slaughter," *Complete Poetic Works of Hayyim Nahman Bialik* (New York: Histadruth Ivrith of America, 1948), 134–35.

60 *"It is good to die for"*: Eli Kavon, *Jerusalem Post*, July 16, 2022, https://www.jpost.com/opinion/article-712277.

62 *0.2 percent:* Pew Research Center, "The Global Religious Landscape," December 8, 2012, https://www.pewresearch.org/religion/2012/12/18/global-religious-landscape-jew/.

5. Antisemitism

69 *coined a distinction:* Solomon Schechter, "Higher Criticism—Higher Anti-Semitism," *Seminary Addresses and Other Papers* (Cincinnati: Ark Publishing, 1915), 35–39.

70 *"Our great claim"*: Schechter, "Higher Criticism," 37.

72 *"a certain perception"*: "Working Definition of Antisemitism," International Holocaust Remembrance Alliance, https://holocaustremembrance.com/resources/working-definition-antisemitism.

77 *"Those who burn books"*: "The Tale of Two Book Burnings: Heine's Warning in Context" (on a lecture by Sholomo Avineri, March 11, 1994), Central European University Newsroom, March 13, 1994, https://www.ceu.edu/article/2014-03-13/tale-two-book-burnings-heines-warning-context#:~:text=Heinrich%20Heine's%20ominous%20sentence%2C%20%22those,century%20history%20of%20German%20Jewry.

6. Grief, Clarity, Solidarity

85   *the face of evil:* India Today, "Audio Reveals Hamas Terrorist
      Bragging to Parents on Call: 'I Killed 10 Jews,'" November 2023,
      YouTube video, https://www.youtube.com/watch?v=Fhl9JFiw6sU.

91   *"cannot approach Hamas":* Amos Oz, interview with Dennis Stute, "For
      Israel, It Is a Lose-Lose Situation," Qantara, January 8, 2014, https://
      qantara.de/en/article/interview-amos-oz-israel-it-lose-lose-situation.

91   *"When people show you":* Joan Podrazik, "Oprah's Life Lesson
      From Maya Angelou: 'When People Show You Who They Are, Believe
      Them,'" *Huffington Post*, March 13, 2014, https://www.huffpost.com
      /entry/oprah-life-lesson-maya-angelou_n_2869235.

93   *"From time to time":* Michael Wyschogrod, "Religion and
      International Human Rights: A Jewish Perspective," *The Formation of
      Social Policy in the Catholic and Jewish Traditions* (Notre Dame: University
      of Notre Dame Press, 1980), 132.

94   *"In the face of abnormal":* Wyschogrod, "Religion and International
      Human Rights," 136.

94   *peace demonstrators:* Aida Edemariam, "A Life in Writing: Amos Oz,"
      Guardian, February 11, 2009, https://www.theguardian.com
      /culture/2009/feb/14/amos-oz-interview.

97   *in this dark hour:* Rabbi Shlomo Jakobovits, "Chief Rabbi Lord Jakobovits
      zt"l," *Jewish Action*, Spring 2000, https://jewishaction.com/jewish
      -world/people/chief-rabbi-lord-jakobovits-ztl/.

7. The Tribal Moment

104 *our tribal moment:* Rabbi Donniel Hartman, "Donniel Hartman:
      Differences Between Genesis and Exodus Jews," audio lecture,
      November 11, 2011, Aitz Hayim Center for Jewish Living, https://
      archive.org/details/DonnielHartmanGenesisVsExodusJews_59.

108 *"Israel has become":* Jordana Horn, "Former ADL Head Abe Foxman:
      'Israel Has Become the Jew Among the Nations,'" *Times of Israel*,
      March 7, 2024, https://www.timesofisrael.com/former-adl-head
      -abe-foxman-israel-has-become-the-jew-among-the-nations/.

9. Kiy'mu V'kiblu

129 *eschew faith commitments:* Pew Research Center, *Jewish Americans in
      2020: U.S. Jews Are Culturally Engaged, Increasingly Diverse,
      Politically Polarized, and Worried About Anti-Semitism,* May 11, 2021,
      https://www.pewresearch.org/religion/2021/05/11/jewish
      -americans-in-2020/.

131 *"When I pray"*: Marc Wolf, "The Question That Matters," Jewish Theological Seminary, April 12, 2003, https://www.jtsa.edu /torah/the-question-that-matters/.

136 *"A community cannot"*: Arthur Hertzberg, *The Jews in America: Four Centuries of an Uneasy Encounter* (New York: Simon & Schuster, 1989), 388.

10. Empathy or Revenge

139 *anger on the streets:* Yitzhak Rabin, "Statement by Israeli Prime Minister Rabin on the 1994 Murders in Hebron" (Israeli Ministry of Foreign Affairs Archive, February 25, 1994), Encyclopedia.com, 2024, https://www.encyclopedia.com/politics/energy-government -and-defense-magazines/statement-israeli-prime-minister-rabin-1994 -murders-hebron.

142 *the assertion "never again"*: Yehuda Elkana, "The Need to Forget," *CEU Weekly* (originally published in *Ha'aretz*, March 2, 1988), August 20, 2014, http://ceuweekly.blogspot.com/2014/08/in-memoriam-need -to-forget-by-yehuda.html.

143 *It was outrageous:* Jacob Madig et al., "Smotrich Says He Didn't Realize His 'Wipe Out' Huwara Call Would Be Seen as IDF Order," *Times of Israel*, March 9, 2023, https://www.timesofisrael.com/smotrich-didnt -realize-wipe-out-huwara-call-would-be-seen-as-idf-order-apologizes/.

144 *"Returning hate for hate"*: Martin Luther King Jr., *Strength to Love* (Boston: Beacon Press, 1963), 47.

11. *Sinat Ḥinam*

148 *"With horror, great sorrow"*: The Jerusalem Report Staff, *Shalom, Friend: The Life and Legacy of Yitzhak Rabin*, edited by David Horowitz (New York: Newmarket Press, 1996), 23.

149 *"I was a soldier"*: The Jerusalem Report Staff, *Shalom, Friend: The Life and Legacy of Yitzhak Rabin*, edited by David Horowitz (New York: Newmarket Press, 1996), 16.

150 *"the narcissism of minor"*: Sigmund Freud, *Civilization and Its Discontents* (New York: W. W. Norton & Company, 2005), 107–8.

159 *the word* teyku: Rabbi Louis Jacobs, *Teyku: The Unresolved Problem in the Babylonian Talmud* (London: Leo Baeck College, 1981).

12. The Day After

165 *a two-state solution:* Gidi Grinstein, "Palestinian Statehood: Do It Right," *Times of Israel*, February 11, 2024, https://blogs.timesofisrael .com/palestinian-statehood-do-it-right/.

166 *"In the history"*: *Quote Investigator*, June 21, 2010, https://quote
 investigator.com/2010/06/21/wash-rental/.

173 *"Make yourself a heart"*: Rabbi David Hartman, *A Heart of Many Rooms:
 Celebrating the Many Voices Within Judaism* (Woodstock, VT: Jewish
 Lights, 2001), 21.

13. The Generational Divide

178 *a national civilization:* Noam Pianko, *Zionism and the Roads Not
 Taken: Rawidowicz, Kaplan, Kohn* (Bloomington: Indiana University
 Press, 2010).

180 *"substitute religion"*: Arthur Hertzberg, *The Zionist Idea: A Historical Analysis
 and Reader* (Philadelphia: Jewish Publication Society, 1997), 625.

182 *"For the Jews"*: Eliezer Goldman, ed., "Right Law and Reality," *Judaism,
 Human Values, and the Jewish State* (Cambridge: Harvard University
 Press, 1995), 231.

184 *easier to exit:* Albert Hirschman, *Exit, Voice, and Loyalty: Responses
 to Decline in Firms, Organizations, and States* (Cambridge: Harvard
 University Press, 1970), 1–5.

14. The Broken and the Whole

190 *power tempered by morality:* Martin Buber, *Land of Two Peoples: Martin Buber on
 Jews and Arabs* (Oxford: Oxford University Press, 1983), 169–73.

196 *"The goal is to ensure"*: Benjamin Netanyahu, "Full Text of
 Benjamin Netanyahu's Eulogy for Shimon Peres," *Times of Israel*,
 September 30, 2016, https://www.timesofisrael.com/full-text-of
 -benjamin-netanyahus-eulogy-for-shimon-peres/.

196 *"the test of a first-rate"*: F. Scott Fitzgerald, "The Crack-Up: A
 Desolately Frank Document from One for Whom the Salt of Life Has
 Lost Its Savor," *Esquire*, February 1936, https://classic.esquire.com
 /article/19360201042.

197 *anxiety about this:* Daniel Gordis, "A Failure of Reimagination?," *Jewish
 Review of Books*, 2019, https://jewishreviewofbooks.com
 /articles/5505/a-failure-of-reimagination/#.

197 *"courage is the most"*: Anne Ju, "Courage Is the Most Important Virtue, Says
 Writer and Civil Rights Activist Maya Angelou at Convocation," *Cornell
 Chronicle*, May 24, 2008, https://news.cornell.edu/stories/2008/05
 /courage-most-important-virtue-maya-angelou-tells-seniors.

15. To Begin Again

201 *"According to Jewish"*: Elie Wiesel, *Messengers of God: Biblical Portraits
 and Legends* (New York: Simon & Schuster, 2013), 32.

ABOUT THE AUTHOR

Elliot Cosgrove is a leading voice of American Jewry and a preeminent spiritual guide and thought leader. The rabbi of Park Avenue Synagogue since 2008, he was ordained at the Jewish Theological Seminary in 1999 and earned his PhD at the University of Chicago Divinity School. He sits on the Chancellor's Cabinet of the Jewish Theological Seminary, where he is an adjunct professor. An officer of the New York Board of Rabbis, he serves on the boards of UJA-Federation of New York, the American Jewish Joint Distribution Committee, and the Hillel of University of Michigan and is a member of the Council on Foreign Relations. Rabbi Cosgrove was honored to represent the American Jewish community at the National September 11 Memorial and Museum during the visit of Pope Francis to New York. A frequent contributor to Jewish journals and periodicals, he is the author of fifteen volumes of sermons and the editor of *Jewish Theology in Our Time*.